CHARLES GOUNOD

CHARLES GOUNOD

CHARLES GOUNOD,
W. HELY HUTCHINSON

9 789356 146914
ISBN: 978-93-5614-691-4

Published: 1896

LECTOR HOUSE

LECTOR HOUSE LLP
E-MAIL: info@lectorhouse.com

Charles Gounod.

CHARLES GOUNOD

AUTOBIOGRAPHICAL REMINISCENCES WITH FAMILY LETTERS AND NOTES ON MUSIC

BY

CHARLES GOUNOD

FROM THE FRENCH BY
THE HON. W. HELY HUTCHINSON

1896

CONTENTS

INTRODUCTION

The following pages contain the story of the most important events of my artistic life, of the mark left by them on my personal existence, of their influence on my career, and of the thoughts they have suggested to my mind.

I do not desire to make any capital out of whatever public interest may attach to my own person. But I believe the clear and simple narrative of an artist's life may often convey useful information, hidden under a word or fact of no apparent importance, but which tallies exactly with the humour or the need of some particular moment.

An everyday occurrence, a hastily spoken word, often holds its own opportunity.

Experience teaches; and that which has been useful and salutary to me may perchance serve others too.

The Author of his own Memoirs must perforce speak frequently, nay constantly, about himself. It has been my endeavour in this book to do so with absolute impartiality. I can lay claim to scrupulous exactness both in detailing facts and in reporting the remarks of others. I have given my candid opinion of my own work, but the fable tells us the owl misjudged her own offspring, and I may well be mistaken in mine.

Should Posterity deem me worth remembering at all, it will judge whether my estimate of myself is a correct one. I can trust Time to allot me, like every other man, my proper place, or to cast me down if I have been unduly exalted heretofore.

My story bears witness to my love and veneration for the being who bestows more love than any other earthly creature—my mother! Maternity is the most perfect reflection of the great Providence; the purest, warmest ray He casts on earthly life; its inexhaustible solicitude is the direct effluence of God's eternal care for His own creatures.

If I have worked any good, by word or deed, during my life, I owe it to my mother, and to her I give the praise. She nursed me, she brought me up, she formed me; not in her own image, alas!—that would have been too fair. But the fault of what is lacking lies with me, and not with her.

She sleeps beneath a stone as simple as her blameless life had been. May this tribute from the son she loved so tenderly form a more imperishable crown than the wreaths of fading immortelles he laid upon her grave, and clothe her memory with a halo of reverence and respect he fain would have endure long after he himself is dead and gone.

CHARLES GOUNOD

I

CHILDHOOD

My mother, whose maiden name was Victoire Lemachois, was born at Rouen on the 4th of June 1780. Her father was a member of the French magistracy. Her mother, a Mdlle. Heuzey, was a lady of remarkable intelligence and marvellous artistic aptitude. She was a musician, and a poetess as well. She composed, sang, and played on the harp; and, as I have often heard my mother say, she could act tragedy like Mdlle. Duchesnois, or comedy like Mdlle. Mars.

Attracted by such an uncommon combination of exceptional natural talent, the best families in the neighbourhood—the D'Houdetots, the De Mortemarts, the Saint Lamberts, and the D'Herbouvilles—continually sought her, and literally made her their spoilt child.

But, alas! those talents which give life its greatest charm and seduction do not always ensure its happiness. Total disparity of tastes, of inclinations, and of instincts seldom conduce to domestic peace, and it is dangerous to dream of trying to govern real life by ideal rules of conduct. The Angel of Peace soon spread her wings and deserted the household where so many influences combined to make her stay impossible, and my mother's childhood suffered from the inevitable and painful consequences. Her life was saddened, perforce, at an age when she and sorrow should have been strangers.

But God had endowed her with a strong heart, a sound judgment, and indomitable courage. Bereft of a mother's watchful care, actually obliged to teach herself how to read and write, she also learnt, alone and unassisted, the rudiments of music and drawing, arts by which she was ere long to earn her living.

During the turmoil of the Revolution my grandfather lost his judicial post at Rouen. My mother's one idea was to get work, so as to be useful to him. She looked out for piano pupils, found a few, and thus, at eleven years of age, she began that toilsome life which in after years, during her widowhood, was to enable her to bring up and educate her children.

Spurred by her constant desire to improve, and by a sense of duty which was the dominant feature of her whole life, she realised that a good teacher must acquire everything that is likely to add weight and authority to her instructions. She resolved, therefore, to place herself under the care of some well-known master, to learn all that was necessary to ensure her own credit and satisfy her conscience. To this end, little by little—penny by penny, even—she laid by part of the miserable income which her music lessons brought in, and when a sufficient sum had been accumulated she took the coach, which in those days did the journey from Rouen to Paris in three days. On her arrival in Paris she went straight to Adam, the professor of pianoforte-playing at the Conservatoire, father of Adolphe Adam, the author of "Le Châlet" and many other charming works.

Adam received her kindly, and listened to her attentively. He at once recognised her possession of those qualities which were to foster and strengthen the interest primarily aroused by her happy facility for her art.

As my mother's youth forbade her residing permanently in Paris, to benefit by a regular and consecutive course of instruction, it was arranged she should travel up from Rouen once in every three months and take a lesson.

One lesson every three months! A short allowance indeed! and one which could hardly have seemed likely to repay the cost involved. But certain individuals are living proofs of the miracle of the loaves and fishes, and this narrative will show, by many another example, that my mother was one of them.

A person destined later on to enjoy such solid and well-earned renown as a teacher of music was not, could not be, in fact, a pupil capable of forgetting the smallest item of her master's rare and invaluable lessons. Adam was himself greatly struck by the improvement apparent between each *séance* and the next. As much to mark his appreciation of his young pupil's personal courage, as of her musical talent, he contrived to get a piano lent her gratis. This allowed of her studying assiduously without bearing the burden entailed on mind and purse of paying for her instrument, which, small as it was, had been a heavy tax upon her small resources.

Soon after this a circumstance occurred which had a decisive influence on my mother's whole future life.

The fashionable pianoforte composers at that time were Clementi, Steibelt, Dussek, and some others. I do not mention Mozart, who had already blazed out upon the musical world, following closely upon Haydn; nor do I refer to the great Sebastian Bach, whose immortal collection of preludes and fugues, "Das Wohltemporirte Clavier," published a century ago, has given the law to pianoforte study, and become the unquestioned text-book of musical composition. Beethoven, still a young man, had not yet reached the pinnacle of fame on which his mighty works have now placed him.

About this period a German musician, named Hullmandel, a violinist of great merit, and a contemporary and friend of Beethoven's, came and settled in France, with a view to making a connection as an accompanist. He stayed some time at Rouen, and while there expressed a wish to hear the performances of those local young ladies who were considered to have the greatest musical talent. A sort of competition was organised, in which my mother took part. She had the good fortune of being particularly noticed and complimented by Hullmandel, who at once fixed on her as a fit person to receive lessons from him, and to perform with him at certain houses in the town where music was carefully and even passionately cultivated.

Here ends all I have to tell about my mother's childhood and youth. I know no further details of her life until her marriage, which took place in 1806. She was then twenty-six years and a half old.

My father, François Louis Gounod, was born in 1758, and was therefore slightly over forty-seven years of age at the time of his marriage. He was a painter of distinguished merit, and my mother has often told me that great contemporary artists, such as Gérard, Girodet, Guérin, Joseph Vernet, and Gros, considered him the best draughtsman of his day.

I remember a story about Gérard, which my mother used to tell with pardonable pride. Covered as he was with honour and glory, a Baron of the Empire, owning an enormous fortune, the famous artist was noted for the smartness of his carriages. While driving about one day, he happened to meet my father, who was walking. "What!" he cried, "Gounod on foot! and I in a carriage! What a shame!"

My father had studied under Lépicié with Carle Vernet (the son of Joseph and father of Horace of that ilk). Twice over he competed for the Grand Prix de Rome. His scrupulous conscientiousness and artistic modesty are best reflected by the following little incident which occurred during his youth. The subject given for the "Grand Prix" competition on one of the occasions mentioned above was "The Woman taken in Adultery." Among the competitors were my father and the painter Drouais, whose remarkable picture gained him the Grand Prix. When Drouais showed him his canvas, my father told him frankly there could be no possible comparison between it and his own; and, once back in his studio, he destroyed his own work, which did not seem to him worthy to hang beside his comrade's masterpiece. This fact will give some idea of his artistic integrity, which never wavered between the call of justice and that of personal interest.

Highly educated, with a mind as refined as nature and study could make it, my father throughout his whole life shrank instinctively from undertaking any work of great magnitude. The lack of robust health may partly explain this peculiarity in a man of such great powers; perhaps, too, the cause may be discovered in his strong tendency towards absolute freedom and independence of thought. Either circumstance may explain his dislike to undertaking anything likely to absorb all his time and strength. The following anecdote gives colour to this view.

Monsieur Denon, at that time Curator of the Louvre Museum, and also, I believe, Superintendent of the Royal Museums of France, was an intimate friend of my father's, and had, besides, the highest opinion of his talent as a draughtsman and etcher. One day he invited him to execute a number of etchings of the drawings forming the collection known as the "Cabinet des Medailles," with an annual fee of 10,000 francs during the period covered by the work. Such an offer meant affluence to a needy household like ours, in those days especially. The sum would have provided ample support for husband, wife, and two children. Well! my father refused point-blank. He would only undertake to do a few specially ordered portraits and lithographs, some of which are of the highest artistic value, and carefully treasured by the descendants of those for whom they were originally executed.

Indeed, my mother's unconquerable energy had to assert itself often before these very portraits, with their delicate sense of perception and unerring talent of execution, could leave the studio. How many would even now have remained unfinished, had she not taken them in hand herself? How many times had she to set and clean the palettes with her own hands? And this was but a fraction of her task. As long as his artistic interest was awake;—while the human side of his model—the attitude, the expression, the glance, the look, the Soul in fact—claimed his attention,—my father's work went merrily. But when it came to small accessories, such as cuffs and ornaments, embroideries and decorations, ah! then his interest failed him, and his patience too. So the poor wife took up the brush, cheerfully slaving at the dull details, and by dint of intelligence and courage finished the work begun with such enthusiasm and talent, and dropped from instinctive dread of being bored.

Happily my father had been induced to hold a regular drawing-class in his own house. This, with what he made by painting, brought us in enough to live on, and indirectly, as will be apparent later, became the starting-point of my mother's career as a pianoforte teacher.

So the modest household lived on, till my father was carried off by congestion of the lungs on the 4th of May 1823. He was sixty-four years old, and left his widow with two boys—my elder brother, aged fifteen and a half, and myself, who would be five years old on the 17th of the following June.

My father, when he left this world, left us without a bread-winner. I will now proceed to show how my mother, by dint of her wonderful energy and unequalled tenderness, supplied in "over-flowing measure" that protection and support of which his death had robbed us.

In those days there lived, on the Quai Voltaire, a lithographer of the name of Delpech. It is not so very long since his name disappeared from the shop-front of the house he used to occupy. My father had not been dead many hours before my mother went to him.

"Delpech," she said, "my husband is dead. I am left alone with two boys to feed and educate. From this out I must be their mother and their father as well. I mean to work for them. I have come to ask you two things—first, how to sharpen a lithographer's style; second, how to prepare the stones.... Leave the rest to me; only I beg of you to get me work."

My mother's first care was to publish the fact that, if the parents of pupils at the drawing-class would continue their patronage, there would be no interruption in the regular course of lessons.

The immediate and unanimous response amply proved the public appreciation of the courage shown by the noble-hearted woman, who, instead of letting her grief overwhelm and absorb her, had instantly risen to the necessity of providing for her fatherless children. The drawing-class was continued, therefore, and a number of new pupils were soon added to the attendance. But my mother, being already known to be a good musician as well as a clever draughtswoman, it came about that many parents begged her to instruct their daughters in the former art.

She did not hesitate to grasp at this fresh source of income to our little household, and for some time music and drawing were taught side by side within our walls; but at length it became necessary to relinquish either one or the other. It would have been bad policy on her part to try to do more than physical endurance would permit, and, in the event, my mother decided to devote herself to music.

I was so young when my father died, that my recollection of him is very indistinct. I can only recall three or four memories of him with any degree of certainty, but they are as clear as those of yesterday. The tears rise to my eyes as I commit them to this paper.

One impression indelibly stamped upon my brain is that of seeing him sitting with his legs crossed (his customary attitude) by the chimney corner, absorbed in reading, spectacles on nose, dressed in a white striped jacket and loose trousers, and a cotton cap similar to those worn by many painters of his day. I have seen the same cap, many years since then, on the head of Monsieur Ingres, Director of the Académie de France at Rome—my illustrious, and, I regret to say, departed friend.

As a rule, while my father was thus absorbed in his book, I would be sprawling flat in the middle of the room, drawing with a white chalk on a black varnished board, my subjects being eyes, noses, and mouths of which my father had drawn me models. I can see it all now, as if it were yesterday, although I could not have been more than four or four and a half. I was so fond of this employment, I recollect, that had my father lived, I make no doubt I should have desired to be a painter rather than a musician; but my mother's profession, and the education she gave me during my early youth, turned the scale for music.

Shortly after my father's death, which took place in the house which bore, and still bears, the number 11 in the Place St. André-des-Arts (or rather "des Arcs"), my mother took another, not very far away from our old home. Our new abode was at 20 Rue des Grands Augustins. It is from that flitting that I can date my first real musical impressions.

My mother, who nursed me herself, had certainly given me music with her milk. She always sang while she was nursing me, and I can faithfully say I took my first lessons unconsciously, and without being sensible of the necessity so irksome to any child, and so difficult to impress on him, of fixing my attention on the instruction I was receiving. I had acquired a very clear idea of the various intonations, of the musical intervals they represent, and of the elementary forms of modulation. Even before I knew how to use my tongue, my ear appreciated the difference between the major and the minor key. They tell me that hearing some one in the street—some beggar, doubtless—singing a song in a minor key, I asked my mother why he sang "as if he were crying."

Thus my ear was thoroughly practised, and I easily held my place, even at that early age, in a Solfeggio class. I might have acted as its teacher.

Proud that her little boy should be more than a match for grown-up girls, especially as it was all thanks to her, my mother could not resist the natural temptation to showing off her little pupil before some eminent musical personage.

In those days there was a musician of the name of Jadin, whose son and grandson both made themselves an honoured name among contemporary painters. Jadin himself was well known as a composer of romances, very popular in their day. He was, if I am not mistaken, accompanist at the well-known Choron School of Religious Music.

My mother wrote and asked him to come and pass judgment on my musical abilities.

Jadin came—put me in the corner of the room, with my face to the wall (I see that corner now), and sitting down to the piano, improvised a succession of chords and modulations. At each change he would ask, "What key am I playing in?" and I never made a single mistake in all my answers.

He was amazed, and my mother was triumphant. My poor dear mother! Little she thought that she herself was fostering the birth of a resolve, in her boy's mind, which was some years later to cause her sore uneasiness as to his future. Nor did she dream, when she took me, a six-year-old boy, to the Odéon to hear "Robin Hood," that she had stirred my first impulse towards the art that was to govern all my life.

My readers will have wondered at my saying nothing so far about my brother. I must explain that I cannot recall any memory of him till after I had passed my sixth birthday; prior to that time I remember nothing of him.

My brother, Louis Urbain Gounod, was ten and a half years older than myself, he having been born on December 13, 1807.

When he was about twelve he entered the Lycée at Versailles, where he remained till he was eighteen. My first recollections of that best of brothers are connected with my memories of Versailles. Alas! I lost him just when I was beginning to appreciate the value of his fraternal friendship.

Louis XVIII. had appointed my father Professor of Drawing to the Royal Pages, and having a strong personal regard for him, he had granted us permission, during our temporary residence at Versailles, to occupy rooms in the huge building known as No. 6 Rue de la Surintendance, which runs from the Place du Château to the Rue de l'Orangerie.

Our apartment, which I remember well, and which could only be reached by a number of most confusing staircases, looked out over the "Pièce d'Eau des Suisses" and the big wood of Satory. A corridor ran outside all our rooms, and looked to me quite endless. It led to a suite of rooms occupied by the Beaumont family. One of this family, Edouard Beaumont, was one of my earliest friends. He ultimately became a distinguished painter. Edouard's father was a sculptor, his duties at that time being to restore the various statues in the château and park at Versailles, which duties carried with them the right of occupying the rooms next ours.

When my father died in 1823, my mother was still allowed to live in these rooms during the annual holidays. This permission was extended to her during the reign of Charles X., that is, up to 1830, but was withdrawn on the accession of Louis-Philippe. My brother, who, as I said above, was a student at the Lycée at Versailles, always spent his holidays with us there.

An old musician named Rousseau was then chapel-master of the Palace Chapel at Versailles. His particular instrument was the 'cello (the "bass," as it was called in those days), and my mother persuaded him to give my brother lessons. The latter had a beautiful voice, and often sang in the services at the Royal Chapel.

I really cannot tell whether old Père Rousseau played upon his violoncello well or ill; what I do clearly remember is that my brother was not proficient on the instrument. But I was young, and my small mind could not grasp the fact that playing out of tune was possible; I thought when an instrument was put into a person's hands, he must produce pure tone. I had no conception of what the word beginner meant.

Once I was listening to my brother practising in the next room. My ear was getting very sore from the continual discords, so, in all innocence, I asked my mother, "Why is Urbain's violoncello so fearfully out of tune?" I do not remember what she answered, but I am sure she laughed over my simple question.

I mentioned that my brother had a beautiful voice. I was able to judge it later on by my own ears. And I can also quote another testimony, that of Wartel, who often sang with him in the Chapel-Royal at Versailles. Wartel studied at the Choron School, and sang at the Opera in Nourrit's time; ultimately he took to teaching, and earned a great and well-deserved reputation in that line.

In 1825 my mother's health broke down. I was then about seven years old. Our family doctor at that time was Monsieur Baffos; he had brought me into the world, and had known us all for many years. Our former doctor, Monsieur Hallé, had recommended him to us when he himself retired. As my mother's work consisted in giving music lessons at her own house all the day long, and as the presence of a child of my age was a source of anxiety and even worry to her, Baffos suggested my spending the day at a boarding-school, whence I was fetched back every evening at dinner-time. The school selected was kept by a certain Monsieur Boniface in the Rue de Touraine, close to the École de Médecine, and not far from our home in the Rue des Grands Augustins. Its quarters were soon shifted to the Rue de Condé, nearly opposite the Odéon.

There I first met Duprez, destined to become the celebrated tenor, who shone so brilliantly on the Opera boards.

Duprez, nine years older than myself, must have been about sixteen or seventeen at the time I speak of. He was a pupil of Choron's, and taught Solfeggio in Monsieur Boniface's school. He soon took a fancy to me when he found I could read a musical score with the same ease as a printed book—much better indeed, I make no doubt, than I can do it now. He used to take me on his knee, and when one of my little comrades made a mistake, would say, "Come, little man, show them how to do it!"

Years afterwards I reminded him of this fact, now so far behind us both. It seemed to come back to him suddenly and he cried, "What! were you the small boy who solfa-ed so well?"

But it was growing high time for me to set about my education after a more serious and systematic fashion. Monsieur Boniface's establishment was really more of a day nursery than a school.

So I was entered as a boarder at Monsieur Letellier's institution in the Rue de Vaugirard, at the corner of the Rue Ferou. Monsieur Letellier soon retired, and was succeeded by Monsieur de Reusse. I remained there for a year, and was then removed to the school of Monsieur Hallays-Dabot, in the Place de l'Estrapade, close to the Panthéon.

My recollection of Monsieur Hallays-Dabot and his wife is as clear and distinct as though they were present here. Nothing could exceed the warm-hearted kindness of my reception in their house. It sufficed to dispel my horror of a system from which I had an instinctive shirking. The almost paternal care they gave me quite destroyed this feeling, and allayed the doubts I had entertained as to the possibility of being happy in a boarding-school.

The two years I spent in his house were, in fact, two of the happiest in my life; his even-handed justice and his kindly affection never failed.

When I reached the age of eleven it was decided that my education should be continued at the Lycée St. Louis. When I left Monsieur Hallays-Dabot's care, he gave me a certificate of character so flattering in its terms that I refrain from reproducing it. I have felt it a duty to make this public acknowledgment of all he did for me.

The good testimonials I brought from Monsieur Hallays-Dabot's establishment gained me a *quart de bourse* at the Lycée St. Louis,[1] which I accordingly entered at the close of the holidays in October 1829. I was then just eleven years old.

The then Principal of the Lycée was an ecclesiastic, the Abbé Ganser, a gentle, quiet-natured man much inclined to meditation, and very paternal in his dealings with his pupils.

I was at once put into what was known as the sixth class. From the outset of my school career I had the good fortune of being under a man who, in the course of the years I studied with him, gained my deepest affection—Adolphe Régnier,

[1] *Translator's Note.*—The system of scholarships in French public schools is quite different from that in vogue with us. In the former country the total value is often split up into fractions and bestowed on a number of students. I do not think this is ever done in England.

Membre de l'Institut, my dear and honoured master, formerly the tutor, and still, as I write, the friend of the Comte de Paris.

I was not stupid, and as a rule my teachers liked me; but I must confess I was very careless, and was often punished for inattention, even more so during preparation hours than in the actual school-work.

I mentioned that I joined St. Louis as a "quarter scholar." This means that my college fees were reduced one-quarter. It was incumbent on me to endeavour, by diligence and good conduct, to rise to the position of half scholar, three-quarter scholar, and finally to that of full scholar, and so relieve my mother of the expense of keeping me at college. Seeing I adored my mother, and that my greatest joy should therefore have been to help her by my own exertions, this sacred object ought to have been ever present with me.

But woe is me! Instincts forcibly repressed are apt to wake again with tenfold fierceness. And so mine did, many a time and often—far too often, alas!

One day I had got into a scrape for some piece of carelessness or other, some exercise unfinished, or lesson left unlearnt. I suppose I thought my punishment out of proportion to my crime, for I complained, the sole result being that the penalty was largely increased. I was marched off to the college prison, a sort of dungeon, where I was to be kept on bread and water till I had finished an enormous imposition of I know not how many lines, some five hundred or a thousand, I think—something absurd, I know! When I found myself under lock and key I began to think I was a brute. The feelings of Orestes when the Furies reproached him with his mother's death were not more bitter than mine when I was given my prison fare! I looked at the bread, and burst into tears. "Oh! you scoundrel, you brute, you beast," I cried; "look at the bread your mother earns for you! Your mother who is coming to see you after school, and will hear you are in prison, and will go home weeping through the streets, without having seen or kissed you! Come, come, you are a wretch; you do not even deserve to have dry bread!"

And I put it aside, and went hungry.

However, in my normal condition I worked on fairly enough, and, thanks to the prizes I won every year, I gradually progressed towards that ardently wished-for goal, a "full scholarship."

There was a chapel in the Lycée Saint Louis, where musical masses were sung every Sunday. The gallery, which occupied the full width of the chapel, was divided into two parts, and in one of these were the choristers' seats and the organ. When I joined the Lycée, the chapel-master was Hyppolyte Monpou, then accompanist at the Choron School of Music, well known in later years as the composer of a number of melodies and theatrical works, which brought him some considerable popularity.

Thanks to the training my mother had given me ever since my babyhood, I could read music at sight; and my voice was sweet and very true. On entering the college I was at once handed over to Monpou, who was astonished by my aptness, and forthwith appointed me solo soprano of his little choir, which consisted of two sopranos, two altos, two tenors, and two basses.

I lost my voice owing to a blunder of Monpou's. He insisted on my singing while it was breaking, although complete silence and rest are indispensable while the vocal chords are in their transitional stage; and I never recovered the power and ring and tone I had as a child, and which constitute a really good singing voice. Mine has always been husky ever since. But for this accident, I believe I should have sung well in after life.

At the Revolution of 1830, the Abbé Ganser ceased to be our Principal. He was succeeded by Monsieur Liez, a former Professor at the Lycée Henri IV., strongly attached to the new régime, and a zealous advocate of the system of military drill forthwith introduced into the various colleges. He used to come and watch us drilling, standing bolt upright like any sergeant instructor or colonel on parade, and with his right hand thrust into the breast of his coat, like Napoleon I.

Two years afterwards Monsieur Liez was superseded by Monsieur Poirson. It was while he was Principal that the various circumstances which decided the ultimate bent of my life took place.

Among my many faults was one pet sin. I worshipped music; the first storms that ruffled the surface of my youthful existence originated with the overmastering passion, which had such paramount influence on my ultimate career.

Anybody who knows anything about a Lycée has heard of the Festival of Saint Charlemagne, so dear to every schoolboy.

One feature of the festival is a great banquet, to which every student who has gained either one first or two second places in the various competitions during that term is bidden. On this banquet follows a two days' holiday, which gives the boys a chance of "sleeping out"—in other words, of spending a night at home—a rare treat universally coveted.

The festival fell in mid-winter. In 1831 I had the good luck to be one of the invited guests; and to reward me, my mother promised I should go in the evening to the Théâtre Italien with my brother, to hear Rossini's "Otello." Malibran played Desdemona; Rubini, Otello; and Lablache, the Father.

I was nearly wild with impatience and delight. I remember I could not eat for excitement, so that my mother said to me at dinner, "If you don't eat your dinner I won't let you go to the opera," and forthwith I began to consume my victuals, in a spirit of resignation at all events.

We had dined early that evening, as we had no reserved seats (this would have been far too costly), and we had to be at the opera house before the doors were opened, with the crowd of people who waited on the chance of finding a couple of places untaken in the pit. Even this was a terrible expense to my poor mother, as the seats cost 3 frs. 75 c. each.

It was bitterly cold; for two mortal hours did Urbain and I wait, stamping our frozen toes, for the happy moment when the string of people began to move past the ticket office window.

We got inside at last. Never shall I forget my first sight of the great theatre, the curtain and the brilliant lights. I felt as if I were in some temple, as if a heavenly vision must shortly rise upon my sight.

At last the solemn moment came. I heard the stage-manager's three knocks, and the overture began. My heart was beating like a sledge-hammer.

Oh, that night! that night! what rapture, what Elysium! Malibran, Rubini, Lablache, Tamburini (he sang Iago); the voices, the orchestra! I was literally beside myself.

I left that theatre completely out of tune with the prosaic details of my daily life, and absolutely wedded to the dream which was to be the very atmosphere and fixed ideal of my existence.

That night I never closed my eyes; I was haunted, "possessed;" I was wild to write an "Otello" myself!

I am ashamed to say my work in school betrayed my state of mind. I scamped my duties in every possible way; I used to dash off my exercises without making any draft, so as to gain more time to give to musical composition, my favourite occupation—the only one worth attention, as it seemed to me. Many were the tears and heavy the troubles that resulted. One day, the master on duty, seeing me scribbling away on music paper, came and asked for my work. I handed him my fair copy. "And where is your rough draft?" said he. As I hadn't got one to show, he snatched my music paper and tore it up. Of course I objected, and got punished for my pains. Another protest, and an appeal to the Principal, only resulted in a repetition of the old story; I was kept in school, given extra work, imprisoned, &c., &c.

This first tormenting, far from having its intended effect, only inflamed my ardour, and made me resolve to ensure myself free indulgence of my taste by doing my school-work thoroughly and regularly.

Thus things stood when I took the step of drawing up a kind of "profession of faith," wherein I warned my mother of my fixed determination to embrace the artistic career. I had hesitated some time, so I declared, between music and painting; but I was now convinced that whatever talent I possessed would find its best outlet in the former art, and my decision, I added, was final.

My poor mother was distracted. She knew too well all an artist's life entails, and probably she shrank from the thought that her son's might be no better than a second edition of the bitter struggle she had shared with my poor father.

In her despair she sought our Principal, Monsieur Poirson, and consulted him about her trouble. He cheered her up.

"Do not be the least uneasy," so he spoke to her; "your son shall not be a musician. He is a good little boy, and does his lessons well. The masters are all pleased with him. I will take the matter into my own hands, and later on you will see him in the École Normale. Do not worry about him, Madame Gounod; as I said before, your son shall not be a musician."

My mother retired, greatly comforted, and the Principal sent for me to his study.

"Well, little man," said he, "what is this I hear? You want to be a musician?"

"Yes, sir."

"But what are you dreaming of? A musician has no real position at all!"

"What, sir! Is it not a position in itself to be able to call oneself Mozart or Rossini?" Fourteen-year-old boy as I was, I felt a glow of indignant pride.

The Principal's face changed at once.

"Oh! you look at it in that way, do you? Very well. Let us see if you have the making of a musician in you. I have had a box at the Opera for over ten years, so I am a pretty fair judge."

He opened a drawer, took out a sheet of paper, and wrote down some lines of poetry.

"Take this away," he said, "and set it to music for me."

Full of delight, I took my leave and went back to the class-room. On the way I devoured the poetry he had given me, with feverish haste. It was the romance from "Joseph"—"À peine au sortir de l'enfance," &c.

I had never heard of "Joseph" nor of Méhul, so I had no reminiscences to confuse me or make me fear I might fall into plagiarism. My profound indifference to Latin exercises, at this rapturous moment, may well be imagined.

By the next play hour my ballad was set to music, and I hurried with it to the Principal's room.

"Well! what's the matter, my boy?"

"I have finished the ballad, sir."

"What! already?

"Yes, sir."

"Let me see—now sing it through to me."

"But, sir, I want a piano for the accompaniment."

(I knew there was one in the next room, on which Monsieur Poirson's daughter was learning music.)

"No, never mind; I don't want a piano."

"Yes, sir, but I do, because of my harmonies."

"Your harmonies! what harmonies? Where are they?"

"Here, sir," said I, putting my finger to my forehead.

"Oh, really! Well, never mind; sing it, all the same. I shall understand it well enough without the harmonies."

I saw there was no way out of it, so I sang it through.

Before I got half-way through the first verse I saw my judge's eye soften. Then I took courage—I felt myself winning the game—I went on boldly, and when I had finished, the Principal said—

"Come, we will go to the piano."

My triumph was certain. I was sure of all my weapons. I sang my little ballad over again, and at length poor Monsieur Poirson, completely beaten, took my face in his hands, kissed me with tears in his eyes, and said—

"Go on, my boy; you *shall* be a musician!"

My dear mother had acted prudently. Her opposition had been dictated by her maternal solicitude, but the danger of consenting too precipitately to my desire was outweighed by the heavy responsibility of perhaps impeding my natural vocation. The Principal's encouragement robbed my mother's objections of their chief support, and herself of the aid she had most reckoned upon to make me change my mind. The assault had been delivered. The siege had begun. It was time to capitulate. But she held out as long as she could, and, in her dread of yielding too soon and too easily to my prayers, she betook herself to the following plan, as her final resource.

There then lived in Paris a German named Antoine Reicha, who had the highest possible reputation as a theoretical musician. Besides being Professor of Composition at the Conservatoire (of which Cherubini was at that time Director), Reicha received private pupils in his own home. My mother thought of placing me under him to study harmony, counterpoint, and fugue—the elements of the art of composition, in fact. She therefore asked the Principal's permission to take me to him on Sundays during the boys' walking hour. As the time spent in going to and from Reicha's house, added to that spent over my lesson, practically covered the same period as the boys' airing, my regular studies were not likely to be interfered with by this special favour.

The Principal gave his consent, and my mother took me to Reicha's house. But, before she handed me over to him, she thus (as she told me herself long afterwards) addressed him privately—

"My dear Monsieur Reicha, I bring you my son, a mere child, who desires to devote himself to musical composition. I bring him against my own judgment; I dread an artist's life for him, knowing, as I do, the many difficulties which beset it. But I will not ever reproach myself, nor let my son reproach me, with having hindered his career, or spoilt his happiness. I want to make quite sure, before all else, that his talent is real and his vocation true. And so I beg you will put him to the severest test. Place everything that is most difficult before him. If he is destined to be a true artist, no trouble will discourage him; he will triumph over it all. If, on the other hand, he loses heart, I shall know where I am; and shall certainly not allow him to embark on a career, the first obstacles in which he has not energy to overcome."

Reicha promised my mother I should be treated as she wished; and he kept his word, as far as in him lay.

As samples of my boyish talent, I had brought him a few sheets of manuscript music—ballads, preludes, scraps of valses, and so forth,—the musical trifles my boyish brain had woven.

After looking them over, Reicha said to my mother, "This child already knows a good deal of what I shall have to teach him, but he is unconscious of the knowledge he possesses."

In a year or two I had reached a point in my harmony studies which was rather beyond the elementary stage—counterpoint of all kinds, for instance, fugues, canons, &c. My mother then asked him—

"Well, what do you think of him?"

"I think, my dear lady, that it is no use trying to stop him; nothing disheartens him. He finds pleasure and interest in everything; and what I like best about him is, he always wants to know the 'reason why.'"

"Well," said my mother, "I suppose I must give in."

I knew right well there was no trifling with her. Often she would say to me—

"You know, if you don't get on well, round comes a cab, and off you go to the notary." The very idea of a notary's office was enough to make me do miracles.

But, anyhow, my college reports were good; and though I was threatened with extra work to make up for lost time, I took good care the masters should have no cause to complain that my music interfered with my other studies.

Once indeed I was punished, and pretty sharply too, for having left some work or other unfinished. The master had given me a heavy imposition, 500 lines or thereabouts to write out. I was writing away (or rather I was scribbling with the careless haste which is usually bestowed on such a task) when the usher on duty came to the table. He watched me silently for some minutes, then laid his hand quietly on my shoulder and said—

"You know you are writing dreadfully badly."

I looked up and answered, "You surely don't think I'm doing it for pleasure, do you?"

"It only bores you because you do it badly." He went on quietly, "If you took a little more trouble about it, it would bore you less."

The simple, sensible words, and the gentle and persuasive kindness which marked their quiet utterance, made such an impression on me, that I do not think I ever offended again by negligence or inattention to my work. They brought me a sudden revelation, as complete as it was precise, of what diligence and attention really mean. I returned to my imposition, and finished it in a very different frame of mind. The irksomeness of the task was lost in the satisfaction and benefit of the good advice I had been given.

Meanwhile my musical studies bore good fruit, and daily grew more and more absorbing.

My mother seized the opportunity of a vacation of some days' duration, the New Year's holidays, to give me what was at once a great pleasure and an exceedingly precious lesson.

Mozart's "Don Giovanni" was being played at the Théâtre Italien, and thither she took me herself. The exquisite evening I spent with her, in that small box on the fourth tier, remains one of my most precious and delicious memories. I am not certain of being right, but I think it was by Reicha's advice that my mother took me to hear "Don Giovanni."

When I look back on the emotion that masterpiece roused within me, I feel inclined to doubt whether my pen is capable of describing it, not indeed faithfully—that were impossible—but even so as to give some faint conception of what I felt during those matchless hours, whose charm still lingers with me, as in some luminous vision, some revelation of hidden glory.

The first notes of the Overture, with the solemn and majestic chords out of the Commendatore's final scene, seemed to lift me into a new world. I was chilled by a sensation of actual terror; but when I heard that terrible threatening roll of ascending and descending scales, stern and implacable as a death-warrant, I was seized with such shuddering fear, that my head fell upon my mother's shoulder, and, trembling in the dual embrace of beauty and of horror, I could only murmur—

"Oh, mother, what music! that is real music indeed!"

Rossini's "Otello" had awakened the germs of my musical instinct; but the effect "Don Giovanni" had on me was very different in its nature and results. I think the two impressions might be said to differ in the same way as those produced on the mind of a painter called from the study of the Venetian masters to the contemplation of the works of Raphael, of Leonardo da Vinci, or of Michael Angelo.

Rossini taught me the purely sensuous rapture music gives; he charmed and enchanted my ear. Mozart, however, did more; to this enjoyment, already so utterly perfect from a musical and sensuous point of view, he added the deep and penetrating influence of the most absolute purity united to the most consummate beauty of expression. I sat in one long rapture from the beginning of the opera to its close.

The pathetic accents of the trio at the death of the Commendatore, and of Donna Anna's lamentation over her father's corpse, Zerlina's fascinating numbers, and the consummate elegance of the trio of the Masks and of that which opens the second act, under Zerlina's window—the whole opera, in fact (for in such an immortal work every page deserves mention), gave me a sense of blissful delight such as can only be conferred by those supremely beautiful works which command the admiration of all time, and serve to mark the highest possible level of æsthetic culture.

This visit to the Opera was the most treasured New Year's gift my childhood ever knew; and later on, when I won the Grand Prix de Rome, my dear mother's present to me, in memory of my success, was the score of "Don Giovanni."

That year was, indeed, particularly propitious to the development of my musical taste. After hearing "Don Giovanni," I went in Holy Week to two sacred concerts given by the Conservatoire Concert Society, which Habeneck then directed. At the first, Beethoven's "Pastoral Symphony" was played; at the other, the "Choral Symphony" by the same master. This added fresh impulse to my musical ardour. I remember clearly how these two performances, besides giving me an inkling of the proud and fearless personality of that mighty and unrivalled genius, left an instinctive feeling with me that the composer's language, if I may call it so, was closely akin, in many ways at least, to that I had first listened to in "Don Giovanni."

Something told me that these two great talents, each so peerless in its way, came of a common stock, and professed the same musical dogma.

Meanwhile my school life was slipping away. My mother had not yet given up the hope that I might change my mind. She had reckoned on the lengthening of my school hours to have that effect; but failing this, she counted on finally dissuading me by telling me that if I drew an unfavourable number at the conscription I should have to serve, as she was too poor to pay a substitute.

This was a transparent subterfuge. The poor dear woman, who had often enough eaten a crust herself so that her children might be filled, would sooner have sold the very bed she lay on than part with one of us. So, being old enough to understand and appreciate the gratitude and love I owed her for such a life of devoted labour and self-sacrifice, I answered, when she mentioned the conscription to me—

"All right, mother dear; don't let us talk about it. I will see to it myself. I will win the Grand Prix de Rome, and buy *myself* off."

I was at that time in the third class at the Lycée. A little incident which had just occurred in school had gained me a certain amount of respect amongst my comrades.

Our form master was a Monsieur Roberge, who was desperately fond of Latin verses. To write good ones was a certain means of getting into his good books. Some schoolboy trick had been played on him one day, and as the delinquent would not confess, nor any other boy tell of him, Monsieur Roberge stopped the whole class's leave. As the Easter vacation, which meant four or five days' holiday, was at hand, this was a terrible punishment indeed. Nevertheless, schoolboy honour stood firm, and the name of the culprit was not divulged.

The idea struck me that if I were to attack Monsieur Roberge on his weak point, he might relent.

Without a word to my comrades, I wrote a copy of Latin verses, taking for my theme the sufferings of the caged bird, far from the country and the woods, cut off from the bright sun and the free air, and plaintively crying out for liberty. Good luck attended me—I suppose because my object was so meritorious!

When we got back into school, I seized an opportunity, when Monsieur

Roberge's back was turned, to lay my little effusion on his desk. On taking his seat he saw the paper, opened it, and began to read.

"Gentlemen," he said, "who wrote these lines?"

I held up my hand.

"They are extremely good," said he. Then, after a moment, "I cancel the punishment inflicted on this class; you can thank your comrade Gounod for earning your liberty by his good work."

Unnecessary to describe the civic honours showered on me in return.

At length I got into the second class, and found myself once again under my beloved former master, Adolphe Régnier, who had taught me while I was in the sixth.

Among my new comrades were Eugène Despois, afterwards a brilliant pupil at the École Normale, and a well-known classic, Octave Ducros de Sixt, and Albert Delacourtie, the high-minded and clever lawyer, still one of my closest and most faithful friends. We four practically monopolised the top places, the "Banc d'Honneur."

At Easter I was considered sufficiently advanced to warrant my being transferred to the Rhetoric class;[2] but I only remained in it three months, as my studies had been sufficiently satisfactory for my mother finally to abandon her idea of extra classes.

I left the Lycée at the summer vacation, being then a little over seventeen.

Still I had not passed through the Philosophy class, and my mother had no intention of allowing me to leave my education incomplete. It was therefore agreed and arranged that I was to go on working at home, and, without interrupting my musical studies, to read for my Bachelor of Arts degree, which I succeeded in taking within the year.

I have often regretted that I did not take a science degree as well. I should thus have made acquaintance at an early age with many ideas whose importance I only realised later in life, and my ignorance of which I much regret. But time was running short. I had to set to work if I was to win the Grand Prix de Rome, as I had promised; it was a matter of life or death for my career. So there was not a moment to be lost.

Reicha being just dead, I was bereft of my instructor. The idea of taking me to Cherubini, and asking him to put me into one of the composition classes at the Conservatoire, struck my mother. I took some of my exercise books under my arm, to give Cherubini some notion of what Reicha had taught me. But he did not think fit to look at them. He questioned me closely about my past, and as soon as he knew I had been a pupil of Reicha's (although the latter had been a colleague of his at the Conservatoire), he said to my mother—

[2] In French public schools the upper classes are not referred to by numbers. Thus the first or highest class is "Philosophy," the second "Rhetoric," and so on. (See also *post*, in text.)

"Very well; now he must begin all over again. I don't approve of Reicha's style. He was a German, and this boy ought to follow the Italian method. I shall put him under my pupil Halévy, to work at counterpoint and fugue."

Cherubini's view was that the Italian school followed the only orthodox system of music, as laid down by Palestrina, whereas the Germans look upon Sebastian Bach as the high priest of harmony.

Far from being discouraged by this decision, I was only too delighted.

"All the better," said I to myself; and to my mother, later on, "It will be great advantage to me. I can choose the best points of both the great schools. It is all for the best."

I joined Halévy's class, and at the same time Cherubini put me into the hands of Berton, the author of "Montano and Stéphanie," and a varied collection of other works of high value, who was to instruct me in lyrical composition.

Berton was a man of quick wit, kindly and refined. He was a great admirer of Mozart, whose works he constantly recommended to the attention of his old pupils.

"Study Mozart," he was always saying; "study the 'Nozze de Figaro!'"

He was quite right. That work should be every musician's text-book. Mozart bears the same relation to Palestrina and Bach as the New Testament bears to the Old, in Holy Writ.

When Berton died, as he did a couple of months after I joined his class, Cherubini handed me over to Le Sueur, the composer of "Les Bardes," "La Caverne," and of many masses and oratorios.

He was a man of grave and reserved character, but fervent and almost biblical in inspiration, and devoted to sacred subjects. He looked like an old patriarch, with his tall figure and waxen complexion.

Le Sueur received me with the greatest kindness, almost amounting to paternal tenderness; he was very affectionate and warm-hearted. I was only under him, I regret to say, for nine or ten months; but the period, short as it was, was of incalculable benefit to me. The wise and high-minded counsels he bestowed on me entitle him to an honoured place in my memory and my grateful affection.

Under Halévy's guidance I re-learned the whole theory and practice of counterpoint and fugue; but although I worked hard, and gained my master's approval, I never won a prize at the Conservatoire. My one and constant aim was that Grand Prix de Rome, which I had sworn to win at any cost.

I was nearly nineteen when I first competed for it. I got the second prize.

On the death of Le Sueur I continued to study under Paër, his successor as Professor of Composition.

I tried again the following year. My poor mother was torn between hope and fear. This time it must be either the Grand Prix or nothing! Alas! it was the latter; and I was just twenty, the age when my military service was due.

However, the fact of my having won the second prize the year before entitled me to twelve months' grace, and gave me the chance of making a third and last effort.

To make up for my disappointment, my mother took me for a month's tour in Switzerland. She was as bright and active then, at eight-and-fifty, as any other woman of thirty. As I had never been outside Paris, except to Versailles, Rouen, and Havre, this tour was a dream of delight to me. Geneva, Chamounix, the Oberland, the Righi, the Lakes, the journey home by Bâle, successively claimed my admiration. We went through the whole of Switzerland on mule-back, rising early, going late to rest; and my mother was always up and ready dressed before she roused me.

I returned to Paris full of fresh zeal for my work, and quite determined this time to carry off the Grand Prix de Rome.

At last the period of competition came round. I entered, and I won the prize.

My poor mother wept for joy, first of all, but afterwards at the thought that the first result of my triumph would be to separate us for three weary years, two of which I should have to spend in Rome and one in Germany. We had never been parted before, and now her daily life was going to be like the story of the "Two Pigeons."

The winners of the other Grand Prizes of my year were Hébert for painting, Gruyère for sculpture, Lefuel for architecture, and Vauthier (grandson of Galle) for medal engraving.

Towards the end of October the different prizes were publicly awarded with becoming solemnity. This ceremony was an annual function, one of its features being the performance of the cantata which had won the music prize. My brother, who was an architect, had highly distinguished himself at the École des Beaux Arts under the teaching of Huyot. Whether it was that he foresaw his younger brother would one day win a Grand Prix, and consequently have to go abroad to study, I know not, but Urbain utterly refused to compete for a similar honour himself. He did not choose to leave a mother he adored, and of whom he was the prop and support for five long years. But he did carry off a prize known as the Departmental Prize, conferred on the student who has won the greatest number of medals during his attendance at the École des Beaux Arts.

The winner of this prize was publicly named at a general sitting of the Institute, and my proud mother had the satisfaction of seeing both her sons honoured in the same day.

I have already mentioned that my brother was educated at the Versailles Lycée. There he became acquainted with Lefuel, whose father was architect at the Palace, and who was to live to add lustre to the name he bore. They met again as fellow-pupils in the office of Huyot, one of the architects of the Arc de Triomphe, and there became, and always continued, the firmest of friends. Lefuel was nearly nine years older than I. My mother, who loved him like her own son, urgently begged him to look after me; and, in duty to the memory of my good old friend,

I chronicle the faithful care and watchfulness with which he performed his trust.

Before I started abroad I was offered a piece of work, considerable enough at any age, but doubly so at mine. Dietsch, the chapel-master of St. Eustache, who at that time was chorus-master at the Opera, said to me one day—

"Why don't you write a mass before going to Rome? If you will compose one, I will have it sung at St. Eustache."

A mass! of my composition! and at St. Eustache! I thought I must be dreaming!

I had five months before me, so I set to work at once. Thanks to my mother's industrious help in copying the orchestral parts (we were too poor to afford a copyist), all was ready on the appointed day. A mass with full orchestra—think of that!

I dedicated this work—over-boldly perhaps, but certainly with deep gratitude—to the memory of my beloved and regretted master, Le Sueur, and I myself conducted the performance at St. Eustache.

My mass, I readily admit, was a work of no very remarkable value. The novice's inexperience in the art of handling an orchestra with all its varied tints of sound, which needs so long a practical experience, was all too apparent. As to the musical ideas my work contained, their value was confined to a fairly clear conception of the sense of its sacred subject, and a tolerably close harmony between that sense and the music intended to illustrate it. But vigour of design and general outline were sorely lacking.

However that may have been, this first attempt brought me much kind encouragement; the following, for instance, which touched me specially.

Returning home with my mother after the performance of the mass, I found a messenger with a note awaiting me at the door of our apartment (then at 8 Rue de l'Éperon, on the ground floor). I opened the letter, and read as follows:—

"Well done, young fellow, whom I remember as a child! All honour to your 'Gloria,' your 'Crédo,' and, above all, your 'Sanctus.' It is fine, it is full of religious feeling! Well done, and many thanks! You have made me very happy!"

It was from good Monsieur Poirson, my former Principal at Saint Louis, then Principal of the Lycée Charlemagne. He had seen the announcement of my mass, and had come with all speed to witness the first public appearance of the young artist to whom he had said, seven years before, "Go on, my boy; you *shall* be a musician!"

I was so touched by his kindly thought, that I did not even wait to go indoors. I rushed into the street, called a cab, and hurried to the Lycée Charlemagne, in the Rue St. Antoine, where I found my dear old Principal, who clasped me to his heart.

I had only four more days to spend with my mother before leaving her for three years. She, poor woman, through her constant tears, was getting everything ready against the day of my departure. Very soon it came.

II

ITALY

WE left Paris, Lefuel and Vauthier and I, on December 5th, 1839, by the mail-coach which started from the Rue Jean Jacques Rousseau.

My brother was the only person there to bid us farewell. Our first stage took us to Lyons. Thence we followed the course of the Rhône, by Avignon, Arles, &c., till we reached Marseilles.

At Marseilles we took a "vetturino."

"Vetturino!" What memories the word recalls! Alas for the poor old travelling carriage long since shouldered out of existence, crushed and smothered under the hurrying feet of the iron horse!

The good-natured old conveyance which one stopped at will, whenever one wanted peacefully to admire those beautiful bits of scenery through or mayhap underneath which the snorting steam horse, devouring space like any meteor, now whisks you like a parcel! In those days men travelled gradually, insensibly from one impression to another; now this railway mortar fires us from Paris, in our sleep, to wake under some Eastern sky. No imperceptible mental transition or climatic change! We are shot out roughly, treated as a British merchant treats his merchandise. Close packed like bales down in a hold, and delivered with all speed, like fish sent on by express train to make sure of its arriving fresh! If only progress, that remorseless conqueror, would even spare its victims' lives! But no, the vetturino has departed utterly. Yet I bless his memory. But for his aid, I should have never had the joy of seeing that wonderful Corniche, the ideal introduction to the delicious climate and the picturesque charms of Italy—Monaco, Mentone, Sestri, Genoa, Spezzia, Trasimeno, Tuscany, Pisa, Lucca, Sienna, Perugia, Florence. A progressive and many-sided education, Nature's explanation of the existence of the great masters, while they in turn teach man to look at Nature. For close on two happy months we dallied over all this loveliness, leisurely tasting and enjoying it, till finally, on January 27th, 1840, we entered the great city which was to be our home, our teacher, our initiator into the noblest and severest beauties of nature and of art.

The Director of the French Academy at that time was Monsieur Ingres. He had been one of my father's early friends. On our arrival, we called, as in duty bound, to pay him our respects. As soon as he saw me he cried—

"You are Gounod, I am sure! Goodness! how like your father you are!"

He spoke of my father's talent as a draughtsman, of his kind disposition, of his brilliant wit and conversational powers, with an admiration which, coming as it did from the lips of so distinguished an artist, constituted the most delightful welcome I could have had. Soon we were established in our different quarters, consisting in each case of a single large apartment, called a *Loggia,* which served alike as bedroom and as studio.

My first thought was of the length of time which must elapse before I saw my mother again. I wondered whether my work as an art student would suffice to enable me to bear with any sort of patience a separation which, between Rome and Germany, must cover quite three years.

Gazing from my window on the dome of St. Peter's in the distance, I readily yielded to the melancholy aroused by my first taste of solitude—though solitude is hardly a word applicable to this palace, where twenty-two of us dwelt, and where we all met at least twice daily at the common board, in that splendid dining-hall, the walls of which are covered with the portraits of every student since the foundation of the Academy. Besides, it was my nature to make friends quickly, and live on excellent terms with those about me.

I must admit, too, that my low spirits were in great part due to my first impressions of Rome itself. I was utterly disappointed. Instead of the city of my dreams, majestic and imposing, full of ancient temples, antique monuments, and picturesque ruins, I saw a mere provincial town, vulgar, characterless, and, in most places, very dirty.

My disenchantment was complete, and it would have required but little persuasion to make me throw up the sponge, pack my traps, and hurry back to Paris and all I cared for as quickly as wheels could take me there. As a matter of fact, Rome does possess all the beauties I had dreamt of, but the eye of a new-comer cannot at first perceive them. They must be sought out, felt for, here and there, until by slow degrees the sleeping glories of the splendid past awake, and the dumb ruins and dry bones arise once more to life before their patient student's eyes.

I was still too young, not only in years, but also and especially in character, to grasp or understand at the first glance the deep significance of the solemn, austere city, whose whisper is so low that only ears accustomed to deep silence and sharpened by seclusion can catch its tones. Rome is the echo of the Scriptural words of the Maker of the human soul to His own handiwork: "I will bring her into the wilderness, and speak comfortably to her." So various is she in herself, and in such deep calm is everything about her lapped, that no conception of her immense *ensemble* and prodigious wealth of treasures is possible at first. The Past, the Present, and the Future alike crown her the capital not of Italy only, but of the human race in general. This fact is recognised by all who have lived there long; for whatever the country whence the wanderer comes, whatever tongue he speaks, Rome has a universal language understood by all, so that the thoughtful traveller, leaving her, feels he leaves home behind him.

Little by little I felt my low spirits evaporate and a new feeling take their place. I began to know Rome better, and cast aside the winding-sheet which had enwrapped me, as it were. But even up to this I had not been living in downright idleness.

My favourite amusement was reading Goethe's "Faust," in French of course, as I knew no German. I read too, with great interest, "Lamartine's Poems." Before I began to think about sending home my first batch of work, for which I still had plenty of time before me, I busied myself in composing a number of melodies, among others "Le Vallon" and also "Le Soir," the music of which I incorporated ten years afterwards into a scene in the first act of my opera "Sappho," to the beautiful lines written by my dear friend and famous colleague, Emile Augier, "Héro sur la tour solitaire."

I wrote both these songs at a few days' interval, almost as soon as I arrived at the Villa Medecis.

Six weeks or so slipped away. My eyes had grown accustomed to the silent city, which at first had seemed so like a desert to me. The very silence ended by having its own charm, by becoming an actual pleasure to me; and I took particular delight in roaming about the Forum, the ruins of the Palatine Hill, and the Coliseum, those glorious relics of a power and splendour departed, which have rested now for centuries under the august and peaceful rule of the universal Shepherd, and the Empress city of the world.

A very worthy and pleasant family of the name of Desgoffe was at that time staying with Monsieur and Madame Ingres. I had made their acquaintance, and gradually became very intimate with them. Alexandre Desgoffe was not an Academy student like myself, but a private pupil of Monsieur Ingres, and a very fine landscape painter. Yet he lived in the Academy buildings with his wife and daughter, a charming child of nine, who afterwards became Madame Paul Flandrin, and retained as a wife and mother the sweetness which characterised her girlhood. Desgoffe himself was a man in ten thousand; downright and honest, modest and unselfish, simple and pure-minded as a child, the kindest and most faithful soul on earth. It may easily be guessed that my mother was very glad to learn that I had such good people near me to show me true affection, and not only comfort my loneliness, but, if necessary, give me kind and devoted care.

We students always spent our Sunday evenings in the Director's drawing-room, to which we had the right of *entrée* on that day. Generally there was music. Monsieur Ingres had taken a fancy to me, and he was music mad. He particularly affected Haydn, Mozart, Beethoven, and above all Gluck, whose noble style, with its touch of pathos, stamped him in his mind as something of the ancient Greek, a worthy scion of Æschylus, of Sophocles, or Euripides.

Monsieur Ingres played the violin. He was no finished performer, still less was he an artist; but in his youth he had played in the orchestra of his native town, Montauban, and taken part in the performance of Gluck's operas.

I had read and studied the German composer's works. As to Mozart's "Don Giovanni," I knew it all by heart; so, although not a very good pianist, I was quite up to treating Monsieur Ingres to recollections of his favourite score.

Beethoven's symphonies I knew by heart, too, and these he passionately admired; we often spent the greater part of the night deep in talk over the great master's works, and before long I stood high in his good graces.

Nobody who was not intimately acquainted with Monsieur Ingres can have any correct idea of what he really was. I lived in close familiarity with him for some considerable time, and I can testify to the simplicity, uprightness, and frankness of his nature. He was full of candour and of noble impulse, enthusiastic, even eloquent at times. He could be as tender and gentle as a child, and then again he would pour out a torrent of apostolic wrath. His unaffectedness and sensitive delicacy were touching, and there was a freshness of feeling about the man which has never yet been found in any *poseur*, as some people have elected to call him.

Humble and modest in the presence of a master-mind, he stood up proudly and boldly against foolish arrogance and self-sufficiency. He was fatherly in his treatment of his students, whom he looked on as his children, giving each his appointed rank with jealous care, whatever that of the visitors in his drawing-room might be. Such were the characteristics of the excellent noble-minded artist, whose invaluable tuition I was about to have the good fortune of receiving.

I was deeply attached to him, and I shall always remember his dropping in my hearing one or two of those luminous sentences which, when properly understood, cast so much light upon the artistic life. Every one knows that famous saying of his, "Drawing is the honesty of art." He said another thing before me once, which is a perfect volume in itself, "There is no grace where there is no strength." True, indeed! for grace and strength are the two complementary constituents of perfect beauty. Strength saves grace from degenerating into mere wanton charm, while grace purifies strength from all its coarseness and brutality—the perfect harmony of the two thus marking the highest level art can reach, and giving it the stamp of genius.

It has been said and frequently repeated, parrot-wise, that Monsieur Ingres was intolerant and exclusive. That is utterly untrue. If he had a way of imposing his opinions, it was because of his intense belief—the surest means of influencing others. I never knew any one with such a power of universal admiration, simply because he knew better than most what to admire, and wherein beauty lay. But he was discreet. He knew full well how prone youthful enthusiasm is to fall down and worship unreasoningly before the personal peculiarities of an artist or composer. He knew these same peculiarities—which are, as it were, the individual characteristics and facial features whereby we recognise them, as we recognise each other—are, for that very reason, the most incommunicable qualities about them, and thence he deduced the fact, first, that any imitation of them amounts to plagiarism, and, further, that such imitation must infallibly end in exaggeration, degenerating into absolute artistic vice.

This explanation of Monsieur Ingres's real character will partially account for the unjust accusation of intolerance and exclusiveness levelled against him.

The following anecdote proves how loyally he could abandon a hastily formed opinion, and how little obstinacy there was about any dislike he might chance to take.

I had just sung him that wonderful scene of "Charon and the Shades" from "Alcestis;" not Gluck's "Alcestis," but Lulli's. It was the first time he had heard it, and his primary impression was that the music was hard, dry, and stern. So much did he dislike it that he cried, "It's horrible! It's dreadful! It isn't music at all! It's iron!"

Young and inexperienced as I felt myself to be, I naturally refrained from arguing the point with a man I held in such profound respect, so I waited till the storm blew over. Some time after, Monsieur Ingres referred again to his first impression of this work, an impression which I believe had already undergone some change, and said—

"By the bye! that scene of Lulli's 'Charon and the Shades'—I should like to hear it again."

I sang it over to him once more; and this time, more accustomed no doubt to that striking composer's rugged and uneven style, he grasped the irony and banter in Charon's part, and the plaintive pleadings of the wandering Shades, who cannot get across the river, not having wherewithal to pay the ferryman.

By degrees he got so fond of the scene that it became one of his favourites, and I was often called upon to sing it.

But his prime favourite was Mozart's "Don Giovanni," over which we often sat till two in the morning. Poor Madame Ingres, dropping with sleep, used to be driven to locking up the piano and sending us off to our respective beds. Although he preferred German music, and had no particular affection for Rossini, he considered the "Barbiere" as a masterpiece. He had the highest admiration, too, for another Italian maistro, Cherubini, of whom he has left such a magnificent portrait, and whom Beethoven held to be the first musician of his age; no slight praise from such a man. Well, we all have our tastes; why should not Monsieur Ingres have his? To prefer one thing does not involve condemning everything else.

A chance incident brought me into closer and more frequent intercourse with Monsieur Ingres. Being very fond of drawing, I used often to carry a sketch-book with me in my expeditions about Rome. One day coming back from a stroll, I came face to face with Monsieur Ingres at the door of the Academy. He caught sight of the sketch-book under my arm, and with that bright and piercing glance of his, he said—

"What's that under your arm?"

I was rather confused, and made answer, "Why, Monsieur Ingres, it's a—it's a sketch-book."

"A sketch-book! What for? Do you know how to draw?"

"Oh, Monsieur Ingres, no—I mean—yes—I can draw a little—but only a very little."

"Is that so? Come, show me your book." He opened it, and came across a little sketch of St. Catherine, which I had just copied from a fresco said to be by Masaccio, in the old basilica of St. Clement, not far from the Coliseum.

"Did you do this?" said Monsieur Ingres.

"Yes, sir."

"Alone?"

"Yes, sir."

"But—do you know you draw like your father?"

"Oh, Monsieur Ingres!"

Then he added, looking at me gravely—

"You must do some tracings for me."

Make tracings for Monsieur Ingres! work beside him, perhaps! Bask in the sunshine of his talent! Warm myself in the glow of his enthusiasm! The thought transported me with joy.

So every evening we worked side by side in the lamplight at this most interesting occupation, I drawing as much profit from the study of the masterpieces over which my careful pencil passed as from Monsieur Ingres's delightful conversation.

I made about a hundred tracings for him of original prints, which I am proud to think found place in his portfolios, and some of which were not less than eighteen inches high.

One day Monsieur Ingres said to me, "If you like I will get you back to Rome with the Grand Prix for painting."

"Oh, Monsieur Ingres!" I answered, "I could not give up my career and take up a new one. Besides, I could never leave my mother a second time."

However, as after all it was music I had come to Rome to study and not painting, it behoved me to seriously seek for opportunities of hearing some. Such opportunities were not exactly numerous, and, it must be confessed, not particularly profitable nor useful either. In the first place, as regarded religious music, the Sistine Chapel in the Vatican was the only place where it was possible to hear anything decent, to say nothing of its being instructive. What they called music in the other churches was enough to make one shiver! Except in the Sistine Chapel, and in that called the "Canon's Chapel" in St. Peter's, the music was not merely worthless, it was vile. It is hard to imagine how such a chamber of horrors could ever have come to be offered up to the glory of God within those sacred walls. All the shabbiest tinsel and trappings of secular music passed across the trestles of this religious masquerade. So no wonder I never tried it twice.

I generally went on Sundays to the musical mass at the Sistine Chapel, often in the company of my friend and comrade Hébert.

But the Sistine! How shall I describe it as it deserves? That is a task more appropriate to the authors of what we see and hear there, or rather of what was heard there formerly. For if the sublime though, alas! perishable work of Michael Angelo the immortal, already sorely damaged, is still to be seen, the hymns of the divine Palestrina no longer resound under those vaulted roofs, struck dumb by the political captivity of the Sovereign Pontiff, the lack of whose sacred presence their empty recesses seem so bitterly to mourn.

I went then to the Sistine, as often as I possibly could. The severe, ascetic music, level and calm like an ocean horizon, serene even to monotony, anti-sensuous, and yet so intense in its fervour of religious contemplation as sometimes to rise to ecstasy, had a strange, almost a disagreeable effect on me at first.

Whether it was the actual style of composition, then quite new to me—the distinctive sonority of those peculiar voices, now heard for the first time—or the firm, almost harsh attack, the strong accentuation which gives such a startling effect to the general execution of the score, by the way it marks the opening of each vocal part in the closely woven web of sound—I know not. The first impression, unpleasant as it was, did not dismay me. I returned again and again, until at last I could not stay away.

There are certain works which ought to be seen or heard in the place for which they were written. The Sistine Chapel, which stands unique upon the earth, is one of the spots in question. The Genius who decorated roof and altar-screen with his marvellous conceptions of the Genesis and the Last Judgment, this painter of the prophets, himself a prophet in his art, will doubtless be as eternally unmatched as even Homer or Phidias. Men of that power and stature never have their equals. Each is a being apart from every other. Each grasps a world of thought, exhausts it, closes the book, and that which he has said, no man can ever say again.

Palestrina gives, as it were, the musical translation of Michael Angelo's great poem. I believe the two masters cast a mutual light on our intelligence. The eyes' delight sharpens the oral comprehension, and *vice versâ*, so that one ends by wondering whether the Sistine, with its music and its painting, is not the fruit of one and the same artistic inspiration? Both are so perfectly and sublimely blended as to appear the double expression of one thought—a single chant sung with a twofold voice—the music in the air a kind of echo of the beauty which enchants the eye.

Between the masterpieces of Michael Angelo and Palestrina such close analogy of thought, such kinship of expression exist, that one is almost forced to recognise the identity of the talents—I had almost said the virtues—which each master-mind displays. Both have the same simplicity, even humility of manner; the same seeming indifference to effect, the same scorn for methods of seduction. There is nothing artificial or mechanical about them; the Soul, wrapped in ecstatic contemplation of a higher world, describes in humble and submissive language the sublime visions that pass before its eyes.

Even the very character and colour of the music and painting in question seem to indicate a deliberate renunciation. The art of the two masters is a sort of sacrament, whose outward and visible sign is but a transparent veil stretched between man and the divine and living Truth. Wherefore neither of the two mighty artists attract at the first blush.

Generally speaking, exterior glitter is what charms the eye; but here we have none of that. All the treasure lies beneath the surface. The impression produced on the mind by one of Palestrina's works is much the same as that given by one of Bossuet's most eloquent pages. There is no specially striking detail, apparently, yet one is lifted into a higher atmosphere. Language, the obedient and faithful exponent of thought, leads the mind gently onward, without any temptation to turn aside until the goal is reached and you are on the upper summit, led by a mysterious guide, gentle, unwavering, unswerving, who hides the mark of his footsteps, and leaves no trace behind.

It is this absence of visible effort, of worldly trick, and of conceited affectation which makes the greatest works so unapproachable. The intellect which conceives them, and the raptures they express, are alike indispensable to their production.

But what shall I say of the prodigious, the gigantic talent of Michael Angelo! The amount of genius he heaped up and lavished, both as a painter and a poet, on the walls of this unique building, is beyond anything man can measure.

What a masterly grouping of the events and personages which sum up and symbolise the whole essential history of the human race! What a wonderful conception is that double row of prophets and sibyls, those seers of either sex, whose gaze pierces the darkness of the future, and in whose persons the omniscient Spirit is carried through the ages! What a volume of teaching is that vaulted ceiling covered with the pictured story of our human origin, and whereon the colossal figure of the prophet Jonah, cast out of the belly of the whale, is linked with the triumph of that other Jonah, snatched by the power of His own might out of the darkness of the tomb, and victorious over death itself!

What a sublime and gorgeous Hosanna seems to rise from the legion of angels twisting, as it were, and wreathed in ecstasy about the sacred instruments of His Passion as they bear them across the luminous sky, right up into the highest places of the heavenly glory; while in the lower spaces of the picture the cohorts of the lost stand out, gloomy and despairing, against the last livid gleams of a light that seems to bid them farewell to all eternity. And on the vault itself again, what an eloquent and pathetic reproduction do we see of our first parents' early days! What a revelation in that tremendous creative gesture, which gives the "living soul" to the inanimate image of the first man, thus putting him in conscious relation with the principle of his being! What a sense of spiritual power in the empty space, so significant in its very narrowness, left by the painter between the finger of the Creator and the form of the creature; as though he would bid us mark that the Divine will knows neither distance nor impediment, and that for the Deity desire and accomplishment are but one act.

What beauty in the submissive attitude of the first woman, drawn from Adam's side in his deep slumber, as she stands for the first time before her Creator and Father! How wonderful is the transport of filial confidence and passionate gratitude in which she bends before the Hand which beckons, and blesses her, with such calm and sovereign tenderness!

But even were I to pause at every step, I could touch no more than the fringe of this wondrous poem, the vastness of which fairly turns one giddy. This huge collection of biblical pictures might almost be called the Bible of the art of painting.

Ah! if young people only guessed what an education for their intelligence, what mental pabulum for all their future, this sanctuary of the Sistine Chapel holds, they would spend their days in drinking in its lessons. Characters formed in such a noble school of fervour and contemplation will soar far above any self-interest or regard for notoriety.

It was my duty to study opera, as well the sacred music of which the services in the Pontifical Chapel preserved the best traditions. The operatic repertoire at that date consisted mostly of works by Bellini, Donizetti, and Mercadante. All these, though full of characteristic qualities, and even marked from time to time by the personal inspiration of their authors, were, as their general outline and *ensemble* will prove, little more than parasitic creepers round that vigorous trunk, the genius of Rossini. Neither its vigorous strength nor its majestic stature were theirs, yet it was often hidden, for the time being, under the passing splendour of their ephemeral foliage.

There was but little advantage, from a musical point of view, in listening to these operas. The performances were very inferior to those at the Théâtre Italien in Paris, where the same works were interpreted by the best artists of the day. The stage-management, too, was often literally grotesque. I remember going to a performance of "Norma," at the Apollo Theatre in Rome, at which the Roman warriors wore firemen's helmets and tunics, and yellow nankeen trousers with cherry-coloured stripes. It was utterly ridiculous, and might have been a Punch and Judy show.

Consequently I did not patronise the theatre much, and found I did far better to study my favourite scores—Lulli's "Alcestis," Gluck's "Iphigenia," Mozart's "Don Giovanni," Rossini's "William Tell"—in my own rooms.

Over and above the time I spent in close companionship with Monsieur Ingres during the famous "tracing" period, I had the good luck to get his leave to watch him in his studio. It may be imagined I made the most of the permission. I used to read to him while he was painting, and many a time have I dropped my book and watched him at his work. Thus I had the good fortune to see him resume and finish his exquisite picture "Stratonice," which was acquired by the Duc d'Orléans, and also his "Vierge à l'Hostie," intended for Count Demidoff's gallery.

An interesting incident, of which I was an eye-witness, occurred in connection with this latter picture. In the original composition, the foreground contained, instead of the Pyx with the holy elements, an exquisite figure of the Holy Child lying asleep on a cushion, one hand still holding the tassel with which it had been playing. The exquisite little creature, with its tender plump body, was (or, at all events, seemed to me) a perfect gem, not only in ease and beauty of attitude, but in grace of drawing and charm of colour.

Monsieur Ingres himself appeared pleased with it, and when the waning daylight forced him to stop painting, I left him well content with his day's work. Next afternoon I went back to the studio, and, to my horror, the figure was gone! He had destroyed the whole of his work, and removed every trace of it with the palette-knife.

"Oh, Monsieur Ingres!" I cried in dismay.

"Well, yes," he said; and then again decisively, "Yes, I was right!"

The glory of the divine symbol had come to him as something higher than the bright human reality of the infant figure, and therefore more worthy of the Virgin's adoration of her Son. He had not shrunk from sacrificing a masterpiece to truth.

This noble choice, this disinterested integrity, stamp him as one of those whose privilege and reward it is to enjoy unquestioned authority as a guide and teacher of man.

Among my contemporaries at the Académie de France at Rome were a number of young fellows who have grown famous since those days, among them Lefuel, Hébert, and Ballu the architect, all of them members of the Institut de France at this present time, as well as many others who have either gained distinction or been snatched away by an early death before they could realise their country's hopes. I will instance Papety the painter, Octave Blanchard, Buttura, Lebouy, Brisset, Pils, the sculptors Diébolt and Godde, the musicians Georges Bousquet and Aimé Maillard—all of them sons of that much-abused Alma Mater which, in succession to Hyppolyte Flandrin and Ambroise Thomas, produced Cabanel, Victor Massé, Guillaume, Cavelier, Georges Bizet, Baudry, Massenet, and a host of other eminent artists whose names I might add to this list, already long enough, in all conscience.

We students were often asked to parties at the French Embassy. It was there I met Gaston de Ségur for the first time. He was then an attaché, but, as everybody knows, he afterwards became the saintliest of bishops, and, as I thankfully recollect, one of my best and dearest friends.

Though our headquarters were at Rome, we were allowed and expected to travel about and visit other parts of Italy.

I shall never forget the impression Naples made on me on my first arrival with my comrade, Georges Bousquet, now no more. He had won the Grand Prix for music the year before. We had travelled with the Marquis Amédée de Pastoret, who had written the words of the cantata which had won my prize for me.

It all seemed to me like a vision or a fairy tale. The bewitching climate, which sets one a dreaming of Grecian skies; the sapphire bay, set in its frame of isles and mountains, whose slopes and peaks glow in the sunset with tints so magic and ever changing, that the rarest stuffs and brightest jewels are colourless and dull beside them. All around one the endless wonders of Vesuvius, Portici, Castellamare, Sorrento, Pompeii, and Herculaneum, of Ischia, Capri, and Posilipo, Amalfi and Salerno; and Pæstum, with its splendid Doric temples, once lapped by the blue waters of the Mediterranean.

It was the absolute reverse of the effect produced by the first sight of Rome! Here the charm was instantaneous.

When to all these natural fascinations we add the interest attaching to the museum (the "Studii" or Museo Borbonico), crammed with a unique collection of masterpieces of antique art unearthed for the most part at Pompeii, Herculaneum, and Nola—cities which lay buried for more than eighteen centuries beneath the lava of Vesuvius—the immense attraction this city presents to any artist may be conceived.

I was lucky enough to visit Naples thrice during my residence in Rome, and among the most vivid and striking recollections I took away with me was my memory of beautiful Capri, so wild and yet so smiling, with its rugged rocks and verdant slopes.

It was summer time when I first went there, under brilliant sunshine and in torrid heat. The only possible way of existing in the daytime was either to shut oneself up in one's room and try to get a little coolness and sleep in the dark, or else to jump into the sea and stay there, which I was always delighted to do. The beauty of the night in such a climate, and at that season, is well-nigh unimaginable. The vault of heaven literally quivers with stars like an ocean with waves of light, so full does infinite space appear of twinkling tremulous luminaries. During my fortnight's stay I often sat listening to the eloquent silence of these phosphorescent nights. I would perch myself on some steep rock, and stay for hours gazing out on the horizon, rolling a big stone down the precipitous slope from time to time, to hear it bound and bound till it struck the sea below and raised a ruffle of foam. Now and again a solitary night-bird uttered its mournful note, and made me think of those weird precipices whose horror Weber has rendered with such marvellous power in that immortal incantation scene in "Der Freischütz."

It was during one of these nocturnal rambles that the first idea for the "Walpurgis Night" in Goethe's "Faust" struck me.

I never parted with the score; I carried it about with me everywhere, and jotted down in stray notes any idea which I thought might be useful whenever I made an attempt to use the subject for an opera. This I did not attempt until seventeen years afterwards.

However, back to Rome and to the Academy I had to go. Pleasant and seductive as Naples was, I never stopped there for any length of time without wanting to get back to Rome. A kind of home-sickness would seize me, and I would leave without a shadow of regret the spot where I had spent so many happy hours. In point of fact, and in spite of all her splendour and prestige, Naples is a noisy, shrill-voiced town, restless and riotous. Her inhabitants squabble and talk and quarrel and argue from dawn till dark, and from dark till dawn, on those quays of hers, where rest and silence are equally unknown. Wrangling is the normal condition of the Neapolitan. You are fallen upon, besieged, haunted by the indefatigable persecutions of *facchini*, shopkeepers, drivers, and boatmen, who would think but little of carrying you off by force, and every one of whom offers to serve you for less money than his fellow.[3]

Once back in Rome, I set seriously to work. This was in the autumn of 1840.

[3] See letter from Gounod to Lefuel, dated July 14, 1840.

In spite of her professional duties, which engaged her on week-days from morn till night, my mother still found time to write to me often and fully. She must frequently have cut short her hours of sleep so as to give me this proof of her constant and tender care. The very length of her letters bore sufficient witness to the amount of time, robbed from her nightly rest, she had devoted to them. I knew she had to rise every morning at five, to be ready for her first pupil, who came at six, and that often her breakfast hour was absorbed by another lesson, during which, instead of a proper meal, she would swallow a bowl of soup, or perhaps take nothing but a crust of bread and a glass of wine and water. I knew her daily round lasted till six o'clock every evening, and that after her dinner she had a hundred and one household duties to attend to. Besides, she had many people to write to as well as me, and, what is more, she was a Dame de Charité, and often worked with her own hands to clothe her poor. Nothing but the complete orderliness and method with which she laid out her time could ever have enabled her to do so much; but those two essential and fundamental qualities, without which life can be neither occupied nor useful, were hers in the highest degree.

But she had quite given up that pestilential habit of "paying visits," which simply means wasting one's time from Monday morning to Saturday night in going to other people's houses and wasting theirs; *killing* that time, in fact, which kills those who misuse it with sheer weariness.

And so we were brought up on short but pithy maxims, flung to us, as it were, with the brevity of a woman who could not spare time to chatter. "Waste not, want not," and so forth.

A family friend once said to me, "Your mother is not one wonder to me, but two; I cannot conceive how she finds time to do so much, or all the money she gives away." *I* know well enough how she found both. In her own good sense and powerful will. The more she had to do, the more she did. Just the converse of Emile Augier's clever saying, which has much the same meaning, "I have been so idle, I haven't had time to do a single thing."

Now and again my dear excellent brother would slip a word of good and friendly advice into my mother's letters to me. I stood much in need of it, for steadiness was never my strong point, I fear; and weakness, uncounterbalanced by good sense, becomes a power for evil. Alas! I know too well how little I profited by all his warnings, and I cry, *Mea culpa*.

There is a church in the Corso at Rome, called San Luigi dei Francesi, and served by a French canon and priests. Every year, on the 1st of May (the feast of the patron saint of Louis-Philippe), a musical Mass was performed there. The duty of writing the music for the occasion devolved on the Academy musical prize-holder for the previous year. The year I went to Rome, the Mass (with full orchestral accompaniment) was written by my comrade, Georges Bousquet. The following one, it would be my turn. My mother, fearing my other duties at the Academy would not allow me sufficient leisure to compose so important a work, sent me the Mass I had written for St. Eustache. She had copied it herself from my manuscript score, not caring to let that out of her own keeping or risk losing it in the post.

My feelings when this fresh token of my mother's goodness and patience reached me at Rome may easily be imagined. However, I did not do what she suggested, for I considered it my bounden duty, as a conscientious artist, to try and do still better work (no difficult matter, indeed), and I worked on stoutly at the new Mass I had begun composing for the King's fête-day. I finished it in due course, and conducted it myself.

This work brought me luck, and earned me the kindest of congratulations. To it I owe my life appointment of "Honorary Chapel-master" to the Church of San Luigi dei Francesi. Little did I foresee I should be asked to give a performance of the work and conduct it in person the very next year in Germany. Later on I will detail the consequences of this second performance, and the benefits it brought me.[4]

The longer I stayed at Rome, the more irresistible I found the mystic charm and matchless calm that reign within its walls.

Coming from the jagged, bold volcanic outline of the crater of Naples, the simple, quiet, solemn lines of the Campagna, framed by the Alban, the Latian, and the Sabine hills, Soracte the majestic, the mountains of Viterbo, Monte Mario, and Janiculum, made me think of some open-air cloister, quiet and serene. The village of Nemi, with its pretty lake sunk in a great crater, and fringed with luxuriant vegetation, was one of my favourite spots near Rome. The walk round the lake by the upper road is one of the most beautiful that can possibly be imagined. I shall never forget the beauty of that view, as I had the good luck to see it one lovely day, at the close of which I watched the sun go down into the sea from the heights of Gensano.

But the neighbourhood of Rome abounds in such exquisite scenes, objects of endless pleasure trips for travellers and tourists—Tivoli, Subiaco, Frascati, Albano, Ariccia, and a hundred other places, the happy hunting grounds of landscape painters, not to mention the Tiber, many spots on the banks of which are full of majestic beauty and grandeur.

In this memoir of my youthful days, I must not omit to mention, among the artistic treasures which are Rome's special glory, a set of masterpieces which share with the frescoes of the Sistine Chapel the proud boast of being the glory of the Vatican. I mean those immortal pictures by the painter Raphael, forming the collection known as "Le Loggie e le Stanze." In the Stanza della Segnatura hang the immortal canvases of the "School of Athens" and the "Disputa del Sacramento." These two masterpieces, like many others from this unrivalled painter's brush, are of a beauty which appears absolutely unapproachable.

Yet so irresistible is the ascendency of genius, that this Raphael, this matchless painter whom history has set on the very pinnacle of fame, was himself influenced by Michael Angelo. He felt the mighty Titan's grip, he bowed before the giant's power, and his later works give ocular proof of the homage he paid the

[4] See letter from Gounod to Lefuel, with a postscript from Hébert (dated April 4, 1841), with reference to the performance of this Mass.

sublime and almost supernatural genius that dwelt within that powerful and gigantic brain.

Raphael may be the first of painters—Michael Angelo stands alone. In Raphael's case, power expands and blossoms into charm; in Michael Angelo's, on the other hand, charm seems to subjugate and govern power. Raphael enraptures and captivates, while Michael Angelo fascinates and overwhelms. One paints the earthly paradise; the other, like the prisoner of Patmos, gazes with eagle eye even into the recesses of the bright abode of the Archangels and the Seraphim.

These two great apostles would seem to have been called to stand side by side in the high noontide of art, so that the calm and perfect beauty of the younger might serve to temper the dazzling splendour revealed to the poet-painter of the Apocalypse.

A detailed description of the innumerable art treasures of Rome would be out of place in these recollections, of which the sole object has been to relate the principal incidents of my early artistic career.

In the winter of 1840-41 I had the privilege of seeing and hearing the sister of Madame Malibran, Pauline Garcia, who had just married Louis Viardot, then Director of the Théâtre Italien in Paris; they were, in fact, on their honeymoon.

She was not yet eighteen, and her first appearance on the boards had been a great success. I had the honour and pleasure, in the drawing-room at the Academy, of accompanying her performance of the well-known and immortal air from "Robin Hood." I was amazed by the already majestic talent of this mere child, who then promised to be, and eventually became, a great celebrity.

I did not meet her again until ten years later. It is a curious fact, that at the age of twelve, when I first heard Malibran sing in Rossini's "Otello," I made up my mind to embrace a musical career; *ten* years later, when I was twenty-two, I made the acquaintance of her sister, Madame Viardot; *ten* years later again, when I was thirty-two, I wrote the part of "Sappho," which she created with such brilliant success on the operatic stage, for the same lady.

That same winter I had the good fortune to meet Fanny Henzel, Mendelssohn's sister. She was spending the winter at Rome with her husband, who was painter to the Prussian court, and her son, who was still a young child.

Madame Henzel was a first-rate musician—a very clever pianiste, physically small and delicate, but her deep eyes and eager glance betrayed an active mind and restless energy. She had rare powers of composition, and many of the "Songs without Words," published among the works and under the name of her brother, were hers.

Monsieur and Madame Henzel often came to the "Sunday evenings" at the Academy, and she would sit down to the piano with the readiness and simplicity of one who played because she loved it. Thanks to her great gifts and wonderful memory, I made the acquaintance of various masterpieces of German music which I had never heard before, among them a number of the works of Sebastian Bach—

sonatas, fugues, preludes, and concertos—and many of Mendelssohn's compositions, which were like a glimpse of a new world to me.

Monsieur and Madame Henzel left Rome to return to Berlin, and there I met them again two years later.

Before he left the Academy, Monsieur Ingres was good enough to make me a parting gift, which I value both as a proof of his regard and as a specimen of his talent. He did a pencil portrait of me, sitting at the piano with Mozart's "Don Giovanni" open before me.

I was deeply conscious of the loss his departure would be to me, and of how much I should miss the healthy influence of an instructor whose artistic faith was so strong, whose enthusiasm was so infectious, and whose teaching was so trustworthy and aimed so high. Every art demands something beyond mere technical knowledge and special handicraft, beyond the fullest, nay, the most absolutely perfect acquaintance with and practice in the various processes. These are absolutely necessary, of course, but they are only the tools with which the artist works, the outward form and envelopment of each particular branch. But in each art there is a something, the exclusive property of none, still common to them all, higher than all, in default of which they fall to the level of mere handicrafts. This something, which, itself unseen, imbues the whole with life and soul—this constitutes the art itself.

Art is one of the three great transformations which reality, brought into contact with the human mind, and looked at in the ideal and all-powerful light of the good, the beautiful, and the true, is bound to undergo. Art is neither an utter dream nor an exact copy; it is neither the mere ideal nor the merely real. It is like man himself—the meeting and fusion of the two. It is unity in duality. Inasmuch as it is ideal, it soars above us. Were it only real, it would be below us. Morality is the humanisation, the incarnation of good; science is that of truth, and art is that of beauty.

And Monsieur Ingres was a true apostle of the beautiful. It was the breath of his nostrils; his lectures proved it as well as his works—more so indeed, perhaps; for, as a man with a strong creed is generally a man full of great longings, the very fervour of those aspirations will often carry him far above the ordinary beaten track. From the heights thus gained he shed as much light on a musician's as on a painter's work, ushering us all into the presence of the universal sources of the highest truths. By showing me the real nature of true art, he taught me more about my own than any number of merely technical masters could have done.

Though time allowed of my deriving but little benefit from our invaluable intercourse, yet that little made a permanent impression on me, and left a precious memory to console me for the loss of his actual presence.

In the month of April 1841, Monsieur Ingres was succeeded by Monsieur Schnetz, a well-known painter, whose success and popularity were mostly earned by his qualities of feeling and expression. He was a kind and amiable man, full of mother-wit, very cheerful and cordial with the students. In spite of a pair of bushy black eyebrows, which lost themselves in a thick head of hair and almost concealed his forehead, Monsieur Schnetz's expression was gentle and good-humoured, and he was the essence of a thoroughly "good fellow."

My second and third years at the Academy were spent under his rule. He was very fond of Rome, and circumstances helped him to indulge his preference, for he was Director of the Academy of France three times, and left none but kindly memories behind him.

By rights my residence in Rome should have ended with the year 1841, but I could not make up my mind to depart, and obtained the Director's permission to prolong my stay. I remained at the Academy five months beyond the regulation period, and did not leave it until forced to move by the fact that the state of my finances only barely permitted my getting on to Vienna, where the money for the first six months of the third year of my scholarship was to be remitted to me.

I will not attempt to describe my grief at quitting the Academy, at parting with my beloved fellow-students, and leaving Rome itself, where I felt my affections were so deeply rooted. My comrades accompanied me as far as Ponte Molle (Pons Milvius), and after the most cordial of farewells, I climbed into the post-cart which was to tear me (there is no other word) from my two happy years in that land of promise.

I should have been less down-hearted had I been going straight home to my beloved mother and brother, but I was faring alone into a country of strangers, of whose very language I was utterly ignorant; no wonder the outlook was cheerless and dark to me. As long as I could see it from the road, I kept my eyes on the dome of St. Peter's—the crown of Rome and of the universe—then the hills hid it utterly. I fell into deepest musing, and wept like any child.

LETTERS

I

Monsieur Lefuel, Artist, *Poste Restante, Nice-maritime.*

Rome, *21st June, Monday.*

Dear Good Friend,—As it is much more natural and proper for a child to hasten to answer his father, than a father his child, I will begin by apologising for not having sooner acknowledged your last letter dated from Mantua. But it has been in spite of myself, I do assure you. I have had a great deal of writing to do lately, and it is not finished even yet. It is really quite a business (and something else as well) to have to thank people in writing for an interest they merely express through a third person, and which you cannot acknowledge in the same coin. However, I ought to be thankful, and I must not turn up my nose at the idea of bestirring myself a little. Otherwise people might say, "Well, it's easy enough to rid him of that trouble." Eh, dear boy? So I confide this to nobody but yourself and trusted friends like you.

Let me tell you I have done your commission about that coat of yours, which we had been wandering round and round for ever so long, "getting hot," as they say at hide and seek. It has seen daylight at last, and is none the worse; no ugly creases, nor moth of any sort. Likewise I gave your friendly messages to our comrades, who all wanted to know where you wrote from.... I replied that your letter came from Mantua. Whereupon ensued various conversations, both private and general, anent your specially favoured position, especially since a like favour has been refused to Gruyère, who also applied for leave to travel, and declares he brought very good reasons to support his request. I did not choose to talk too much about you, for fear of heating opinions which were already unfriendly, but I did reply at once to a remark made by a person who shall be nameless, to the effect that it was neither very delicate nor very straightforward on your part, last year, to go to Florence in the first instance, when you had been granted permission, by special favour, to go to Naples.

I combatted that idea with all my might, at the same time refusing to be drawn into a discussion which might have degenerated into a dispute. And then, dear Hector, if you only knew how some people's tempers have altered since you went away! If it goes on, I really believe you will find some individuals with their noses in the air, as people call it. I am not the only person that strikes, and I think it can hardly escape your notice too.

As to myself, in another ten days I shall start for Naples, and I expect to spend six weeks or two months, not at Naples itself, but in the kingdom and the islands. The month of September I shall probably spend at Frascati, so as to get a good look, and a last one, at that splendid Monte Cavi, of which I am very anxious to make some studies. If you write to me, direct to the *Poste Restante* at Naples. I will go and fetch my letters when I am in town, and have them sent after me wherever I may be. I have been making a tour, quite lately, in the mountains near Subiaco, Civitella, Olevano, &c. I saw much that was beautiful, but what interested me most was the Convent of San Benedetto at Subiaco. I saw and felt things there that I shall never forget.

I have had news from home lately. They are all well, and send you affectionate messages. They tell me Urbain had written you to Genoa, so that you might find the letter there on the 15th. I don't know how he makes out you will be at Genoa then, but, anyhow, I fancy his reckoning is at fault. However, the letter had better be there before you than after. You are sure to get it when you leave Milan, or you could, if you liked, have it sent you by some friend. Then my mother says Blanchard has been so excessively kind as to make a small drawing of your portrait for Urbain, which has touched both mother and son immensely. Blanchard, so my mother tells me, has had a bad attack of fever since he got back to Paris, but he is much better now. He has dined with my people several times since his return, and my mother says he is very pleasant, has very nice ways, and she likes him because he strikes her as being very good-natured.

You doubtless know, if you have come across any French newspaper, that our friend, Jules Richomme, has not been admitted to compete for the Grand Prix. I am very much distressed at the news, for his sake and that of his family, who so greatly desired to see him win the Prize and come to Rome. I am sure now to see him in Paris, for even if he won the Prize next year, he would not start until after my return. And how goes your work, my dear fellow? Your portfolios must be getting handsomely filled, methinks! Write me all about it—how you are—what you are doing. Though I'm not absolutely sharp in your line of occupation, I think my eagerness to know about everything that interests and pleases you will rub up my wits to a certain extent, at all events. Anyhow, I put myself into your hands to tell me what you like. So long as it does not bore you nor waste your time, tell on!

Farewell, dear Hector. Keep well, and keep me in your affection—that last being a good work, which shall bring you manifold reward!

Mind you are as exact in giving me your successive addresses as I shall be in sending you mine, during my journey and after it.

I salute you, with all filial fondness.

Ch. Gounod.

II

MONSIEUR H. LEFUEL, *Architect,* *Académie de France, Villa Medicis, Rome.*

NAPLES, *Tuesday, July 14, 1840.*

MY DEAR HECTOR,—I wish I could have written these few lines which I now send you by Murat[5] sooner. But the fact is that up to the present I have barely had time to write a tolerable scrawl to my brother; and here in Naples, where I made some acquaintances three months ago, my first duty has been to go round and pay calls. However, I hope to have more time to spare in future. I have written to Desgoffe also, and would gladly have done as much by our good Hébert; please make all sorts of excuses to him for me. He will certainly hear from me direct one of these days, almost at once indeed, for I am thinking, though not quite decidedly as yet, of starting on Wednesday or Thursday in next week to see Ischia and Capri, returning to Naples by Pæstum, Salerno, Amalfi, Sorrento, and Pompeii. A twelve days' trip or thereabouts.

I hope, my dear fellow, your health has been good since I left,—Desgoffe's as well. I beg he'll see you do not work too hard! It must be very hot now where you are. Here in Naples it is sometimes very close; to-day, for instance, it is overwhelmingly thundery and oppressive, but the sea-breeze is not unpleasant, and as we live almost on the sea-shore, we get the benefit of it, and make the most of its freshness.

Naples (I mean the town, of course) bores me more than ever. I am very curious to see Capri and Ischia, and also Pæstum. Yesterday at long last I went up to the Camaldoli; the view is wonderful, especially over the wide expanse of sea. You know how I love the sea. The longer one looks at it, the better one understands that simple horizontal line beyond which one can fancy infinite space stretching away for ever. To-morrow afternoon at four, if the weather keeps fine, we mean to go up Vesuvius and watch the sunset; we shall spend the night there, to see the moonlight on the bay, and the sunrise next morning. You see our expedition promises to be delightful.

The day before yesterday I had a letter from my mother, forwarded from Rome. If it was you who sent it on, dear Hector, accept my best thanks. My mother and my good brother Urbain send you many friendly messages.

What do you think of Monsieur Ingres's picture? Write and tell me, or else slip a line into Desgoffe's letter, when he answers mine. Address your letters to "La Ville de Rome, Quai Santa Lucia, Naples." If I am not there when they arrive, I shall find them when I get back.

Please tell Hébert that I should much like to have his opinion of Monsieur Ingres's picture as well as yours; although I can hardly expect to hear from him until I write myself.

Give my love to my little brother Vauthier, who will not forget me, I hope.

[5] Jean Murat, a Painter, Grand Prix de Rome.

Tell Fleury[6] how sorry I was not to say good-bye to him before starting, and finally, give all my comrades, individually and collectively, my best wishes, in our time-honoured fashion.

Farewell, dear Hector. I send you my best love, with all my heart too, for indeed I feel our common exile with threefold bitterness out here.—Your very affectionate

CHARLES GOUNOD.

Guénepin[7] will write to you in a day or two. He sends you many friendly greetings. He is a very good fellow, and we have had a pleasant journey, although we have never had more than three or four hours in bed. But that's a trifle. When you write, pray let me know if Desgoffe has sent again to fetch my score of "Der Freischütz" from Prince Soutzo's.

III

MONSIEUR HECTOR LEFUEL, *Poste Restante, Venice.*

ROME, *April 4, 1841.*

BELOVED AND REVERED PARENT,[8]—Your afflicted child has been racking his poor brain to know where he should write to you, and was beginning in fact to have serious doubts of the reality of the affection his ancient relative professes for him. However, he now rejoices to have learnt through Monsieur Schnetz that the undaunted centenarian has removed himself from Florence to Bologna, on his way to Venice as fast as he can get there.

To Venice, therefore, does his son, greatly comforted by the joyful news, indite the following epistle to inform him, firstly, that he himself is in rude health, and secondly, that his musical Mass has had a great success, not only among his fellow-students here, but also among the uninitiated vulgar. The thought of his venerable friend's delight at once occurred to the composer, and was indeed a potent factor in his legitimate joy in his success. He begs to add that he unceasingly deplores the absence of his aged kinsman, the person he naturally clung to most while he was here, and of whom Fate has so cruelly and inopportunely bereft him.

I too have news from Paris, my dear good Hector. My letters are full of friendly messages for you. My mother, why, I know not, was under the impression I should see you again within a month or two; I have undeceived her on that head, and I am very sure she regrets it much. And then you will not have heard the news I have about Urbain, news that gave me a great thrill of joy at first, which changed to deepest disappointment when the end of the paragraph appeared. It was neither more nor less than the idea of his coming out to Sicily and Rome, but it is all off now, and this is why.

[6] Confidential servant, who had then been forty years at the Academy.

[7] François Jean Baptiste Guénepin, Architect, Grand Prix de Rome.

[8] See *La Revue* of June 1, p. 476.

The Marquis de Crillon, who has always taken a great interest in my family, being himself about to travel in Sicily, desired to find a talented and educated artist; a really earnest man, in fact, to keep him company. He thought of Urbain, so calling at our house one day, he laid his plan before my mother. She thanked him for his goodness, told him how deeply she appreciated his kind thought, and seized the earliest opportunity of speaking to my brother. He, after short though serious reflection, made up his mind to accept Monsieur de Crillon's offer. When it came to taking leave of his clients, he saw such long faces everywhere, and the regret at his departure was so general—everybody vowed it would be so impossible to find such delicacy, such integrity, and the other good and estimable qualities you know him to possess, in any other man—that getting away began to look far from easy. But there is more besides. Here is what really put the spoke in his wheel. All his future interests were suddenly threatened with compromise for lack of ten or twelve thousand francs. You will easily imagine that under such circumstances he was forced to stay in Paris. I am very uneasy about this somewhat critical state of things, and wait impatiently for news of what has happened next. I will let you know in my next letter. Poor Urbain, so good a fellow, who has worked so hard! Luckily he has plenty of pluck, and will bear the most unpleasant ordeal bravely, but all the same it is very hard on him.

I had heard, dear Hector, you had written to Gruyère. I was beginning to grow jealous, when Hébert said to me, "Cheer up, it's only about something he wants him to do for him!" So I took comfort in the hope that I should shortly hear from you myself. I must tell you that the proofs of friendly interest shown me by many of my comrades here, and notably our good little painter Hébert, have made me very happy. I have the keenest sense of gratitude for the care and attention with which I saw him listen to the rehearsal of my Mass. No indifferent person would have bestowed them, and it is always a pleasure to be able to mention a case of sympathetic interest. Knowing your affection for Hébert, I rejoice to tell you this, for I feel sure your regard for him will not be lessened on account of that he bears me. His health is as rude as mine, and, like all the rest of our comrades here, he bids me send you many greetings. I am going to see if he is at home, and try to get him to add a line or two at the end of this letter.

Bazin has not yet arrived. I haven't an idea what has become of him. I am rather afraid that, in the enthusiasm aroused by his passage through his native place, his fellow-townsmen may have laid violent hands upon his person, and nailed him on a pedestal, as a statue dedicated to his own glory! They are a hot-headed set at Marseilles, and quite capable of anything of the sort! He might send himself in as the result of his Academy work!

Good-bye, my dear Hector. You know how fond I am of you, so, as the saying is, I salute you on both cheeks and on your left eye likewise. If Courtépée[9] is still with you, tell him I grasp his hand with special fervour. I hope you are full of health and spirits, both of you, and I think if you are having the same weather as we are, you must be doing wonderful good work. Good-bye again, dear friend,—
Yours always, CHARLES GOUNOD.

[9] An Architect—Lefuel's "rapin."

My dear Architect,—I seize the opportunity our good musician's letter gives me, to let you know I am alive. Our great sculptor Gruyère has informed me you are struggling with an accumulation of head colds. I trust the sun that shines o'er noble and voluptuous Venice will thaw the ice winter has piled within your brain!

You had a great success at the Exhibition. Everybody was much struck by your drawings, the Ambassador and his wife most of all. I do not mention my own performances; they are neither important nor well executed enough to be worth writing about. Our celebrated composer's Mass has had a great success, both amongst ourselves and with the general public. It was well performed, thanks to the activity he displayed in shaking up all the old sleepy-heads! If you see Loubens,[10] pray give him my best regards. What have you done with Courtépée? Can you get him up in the mornings when you get up yourself, you early bird?

Farewell! If I can make myself either useful or agreeable to you, command me.—E. Hébert.

Murat absolutely refuses to write even two lines. He says he will write later on.

Charles Gounod.

That is a lie!—Murat.

[10] Former student at the École Polytechnique, a friend of Gounod, Hébert, &c.

III

GERMANY

My natural road from Rome to Germany lay by Florence into Northern Italy, and so eastwards *viâ* Ferrara, Padua, Venice, and Trieste.

Although I did make a halt in Florence, I cannot undertake to give a full description of that city. Like Rome, it possesses an inexhaustible store of art treasures. The Uffizi Gallery with its wonderful Tribune (a very shrine of exquisite relics), the Palazzo Pitti, the Academy, Churches and Convents, all teem with masterpieces. But even here, in lovely Florence, Michael Angelo reigns supreme, from the proud eminence of that wonderful and overwhelmingly impressive Medici Chapel, on which, as on the Vatican at Rome, his genius has stamped its mark—unique, incomparable, overshadowing every other.

Wherever Michael Angelo's hand has been, devoutest attention is instinctively aroused; when the master speaks, all others hold their peace. Nowhere perhaps is the mysterious power of supreme silence more effectually shown than in the awe-inspiring crypt of the Medici Chapel. How tremendous is that figure of the "Pensieroso" standing there motionless like a silent sentinel over death, awaiting the blast of the last trump! What repose and grace, too, in the figure of Night, or rather of Sleep, "that knits up the ravelled sleave of Care," beside the robust form of Day lying bound and fettered as it were, till the last dawn shall come. It is the deep meaning hidden in all Michael Angelo's work, as well as the combination of nature and fancy in the attitudes of his statues, which gives them that intensity of expression so specially characteristic of his mighty genius. The huge proportions of his figures are but a type of the deep bed worn by the torrent of his mighty thoughts, and thus it is that any imitation of a form of art which nothing but his genius had power to fill and quicken is foredoomed to seem both pompous and bombastic. But time and lack of funds forbade my tarrying on my road to Germany, so I can do no more than mention Florence, and the pleasant recollections I took away with me. I passed through the deserted city of Ferrara, and spent a couple of days in Padua to see the beautiful frescoes of Giotto and Mantegna.

During my stay in Italy I had made acquaintance with the three great cities which are the art centres of that favoured land—Rome, Florence, and Naples. Rome, the City of the soul; Florence, the City of the mind; Naples, the home of brilliant sunlight, of wild and dazzling gaiety.

I was about to make the acquaintance of a fourth, which, like the others, holds a great and glorious place in the history of art. For the geographical position of the city has given Venice and Venetian art a distinct and unique character of their own.

Cheerful or sad, sunlit or gloomy, rose-red or deadly pale, smiling or darkly forbidding, each and all by turns, Venice is one perpetual kaleidoscope, a weird mixture of the most contradictory impressions, a pearl, I might almost say, cast into a dark and noisome place. Venice! she charms like any sorceress! She is the native haunt of the most radiant form of art. She has cast a flood of sunshine on the painter's canvas!

Unlike Rome, which waits your pleasure, draws you slowly onwards step by step, until you fall into an utter and never-ending thraldom of admiration, Venice takes swift hold upon your senses, and fascinates you at one fell swoop. Rome is serene and soothing, Venice heady and exciting. The intoxication of her charms is tinged (it was at least in my case) with a sort of nameless melancholy, like a captive's sense of loneliness. Is it the shadow cast by the dark deeds of former days, to which the city seems predestined by its very situation? It may be. But whether it be so or not, I cannot fancy any one staying long in this semi-amphibious City of the Dead without growing to feel half choked and plunged into deep depression. With its sleeping waters lapping in dismal silence round the walls of its old palaces, and its gloomy shadows whence the groan of some murdered noble seems to float, Venice is a city of terror; disaster hangs around her even now!

But yet, in the full sunlight, what can be more fairylike than the Grand Canal, or those glittering lagoons whose waves seem made of liquid light! What vivid power clings to those relics of departed splendour, which seem to call aloud to the blue sky, beseeching it to save them from the abyss that slowly but surely sucks them down, and will end some day by engulphing them for ever!

Rome stands for meditation, Venice for intoxication. Rome is the great Latin ancestress whose conquests are destined to give the world one catholic and universal language—a prelude and a means to another Catholicism, deeper and vaster yet. Venice is a true Oriental—Byzantine, not Greek; she makes one think much more of Satraps than of Pontiffs, of Eastern luxury rather than of Athenian or Roman dignity.

Even San Marco, with all its wonders, is more of a mosque than a basilica or a cathedral; it appeals far more to the imagination than to the deepest feelings of the soul. The splendour of the mosaics and gilding, pouring a stream of dark rich tints from the roof of the dome to its very base, is utterly unique. I know nothing like it either in strength of colouring or powerfulness of effect.

Venice breathes passion, as distinct from love. I was bewitched the moment I arrived, but I left it without the pang I felt on quitting Rome—a sure sign and measure of the impression each city had produced on me.

Naples is like a smile from Greece; the horizon glowing with purple and azure, the blue sky reflected by the sapphire sea, even the ancient name, Parthenope, carry us back to that brilliant civilisation on which nature had bestowed such an exquisite setting. But Venice smiles on the traveller in quite a different way. She is coaxing and she is false, like a feast laid out on the trap-door of a dungeon. This doubtless is why involuntarily I felt more relief than regret when I departed, in spite of the masterpieces of art and the mysterious and magic charm I left behind me.

A steamer bore me to Trieste, where I at once took the stage-coach for Gratz. I halted on my way to visit the curious and wonderful stalactite caverns of Adelsberg; they are like underground cathedrals. Crossing the Carinthian mountains (whose ragged outline I consigned to my sketch-book), I reached Gratz, and then Olmutz. Thence I went on by railway to Vienna, my first stopping place on this German tour which it was my one object to get through as quickly as possible, so as to shorten my exile from my mother's roof.

Vienna is a very cheerful city. The inhabitants struck me as being much more like Frenchmen than Germans. They are full of vivacity, high spirits, good-humour, and gaiety.

I had brought no letters of introduction with me, and I did not know a single soul. I took up my quarters in an hotel until I should be able to find quieter and less expensive rooms. It was absolutely necessary, as I was to make a stay of some months' duration, to cut my coat according to my cloth. A travelling acquaintance had strongly advised me to board and lodge in a private family, if possible; and I soon found an opportunity of putting his advice to a practical test.

Nothing in the world would have induced me to let my mother stint herself to swell my modest purse; even had I felt the least inclined to unnecessary expenditure, the thought of her life of toil would have overcome any such temptation. Board, lodging, and theatre expenses (which last were a necessary item in my musical education) made up the whole of my necessary outlay, and with due care and economy the amount of my scholarship was quite sufficient to cover that.

The first thing I saw advertised on the Viennese Opera posters was Mozart's "Flauto Magico." I rushed forthwith and took the cheapest ticket I could get, for the very top of the house. Modest as it was, I would not have bartered it for an empire!

It was the first chance I had had of hearing that exquisite score, and I was perfectly enchanted. It was thoroughly well rendered. Otto Nicolaï conducted the orchestra. The Queen of Night was very well played by a singer of remarkable talent, Madame Hasselt Barth; the High Priest Sarastro by a celebrated artist with a splendid voice, a first-class method, and a magnificent style—Staudigl himself. The other *rôles*, too, were very carefully performed, and I still remember the sweet voices of the boys who appeared as the three Genii.

I sent in my name (as an Academy student) to the Conductor, and asked if I could see him. He sent for me, and I was conducted to his presence on the stage itself, where he introduced me to the various artists, with whom I kept up pretty close relations from that night out. As I could not speak a single word of German, and as most of them knew little more French, it was not easy to get on at first. While I was standing on the stage, I was lucky enough to make acquaintance, also through Nicolaï, with a member of the orchestra, who spoke French. His name was Lévy, and he was the leading cornet-player. His son, Richard Lévy, then fourteen years old, held the same appointment at the Viennese Opera in later years as his father had before him. He received me in the kindest way, and asked me to call upon him. In a very short time we were firm friends. He had three other children. The eldest, Carl Lévy, was a talented pianist and a skilful composer; the second, Gustave, is now a musical publisher at Vienna; and the daughter, Melanie, a charming creature, married the harpist Parish Alwars.

Through his kind offices, after a few weeks' residence in Vienna, I made the acquaintance of Count Stockhammer, one of the most useful friends I found there. He was President of the Philharmonic Society; and Lévy, to whom I had shown the Mass I wrote in Rome, took me to see him, and spoke of the work in very favourable terms. The Count, with kindly promptitude, offered to have it performed in the Church of St. Charles, by the soloists, choruses, and orchestra of the Society.[11] The day fixed was the 14th of September.

My work seemed to give general satisfaction, a fact of which Count Stockhammer at once gave me the most substantial proof by asking me to write a Requiem Mass—solos, choruses, and orchestral accompaniments—to be performed in the same church on All Souls' Day, November 2nd.

I had a bare six weeks before me. The only chance of getting the work done in time was to toil at it night and day, without rest or intermission. I joyfully agreed to do it, and did not lose a moment in beginning. The Requiem was ready by the appointed date. Thanks to that universal diffusion of musical knowledge which is such a delightful and peculiar feature in Germany, a single rehearsal sufficed to make it all run smoothly. I was particularly struck by the facility with which mere schoolboys read music at sight—as easily as if it were their mother tongue. The choruses, too, were rendered to perfection. Among the soloists was a man of the name of Draxler, still quite young, with a magnificent bass voice. He and Staudigl were the leading basses at the Opera. I heard some years later that Staudigl had gone mad, and died; and Draxler, who took his place, still held it when I went back to Vienna in 1868, twenty-five years after, to produce my opera "Romeo and Juliet."

Some time before the performance of my Requiem, Nicolaï had made me acquainted with an eminent composer named Becker, who devoted himself entirely to chamber music. A quartette party met at his house every week, and Holz, the first violin, had known Beethoven very intimately; a fact which, putting his own talent aside, made him very interesting company. Becker was also considered the most capable musical critic in all Germany at that time. He came to hear my Requiem, and published a *critique* couched in terms of such high compliment as to be an immense encouragement to so young a man as I then was. My score, he said, "though evidently from the hand of a novice whose style is still unformed, and who has scarcely realised whither his powers may lead him, displays a grandeur of conception which is exceedingly rare now-a-days."

This heavy piece of work, undertaken and carried through within such a short space of time, knocked me up so completely that I fell ill with a violent attack of sore throat, complicated with abscesses. Not wishing to frighten my mother, I con-

[11] See letter from Gounod to Lefuel, under date August 21, 1842.

fided the true state of my health to nobody except my dear friends the Desgoffes, who were then in Paris. The moment Desgoffe knew I was lying ill in Vienna he left wife, daughter, and the pictures he was painting for the Salon, without a moment's hesitation, and started off to watch by my bedside and nurse me.

The journey from Paris to Vienna took five or six days at that time. It was now mid-winter, December in fact, and what would have been bad enough in any case at that season, was made far worse by the serious illness my poor friend contracted on the way. When he arrived at Vienna he stood sorely in need of care himself. Yet he spent no fewer than twenty-two days at my bedside, snatching a few moments' sleep on a mattress on the floor, and watching over my every movement with the most motherly care. He only left me and returned to Paris when the doctor had satisfied him that I was completely convalescent.

Such friendship is not often met with; but, indeed, Providence has been more than good to me in that respect.

The success of my Requiem had made me alter my plans as to my stay in Germany, and I determined to prolong my sojourn in Vienna. Count Stockhammer gave me a fresh commission on behalf of the Philharmonic Society. This time it was a vocal Mass without accompaniment, to be sung in Lent in the same church, dedicated to St. Charles, my patron saint. I was glad to take this fresh opportunity, not only of gaining practice in my art, but also of getting my work performed—a rare and precious privilege at the opening of any man's career. This was the second considerable piece of work I did at Vienna, and my last. I left that city immediately after the performance for Berlin, *viâ* Prague and Dresden, in neither of which towns did I stay long. But I felt I must not leave Dresden without visiting that admirable museum which, among other treasures, contains the famous Madonna by Holbein, and that other wonderful Madonna known as the "San Sisto," painted by Raphael's master-hand.

As soon as I reached Berlin I went, according to her request, to call on Madame Henzel. But within three weeks I was seriously ill again, this time with internal inflammation, and that just when I had written my mother that I was about to start homewards, and that we should soon be reunited after our weary separation of over three and a half years.

Madame Henzel at once sent her own doctor to me, and to him I presented the following ultimatum—

"Sir, I have a mother waiting for me in Paris, counting the hours till I get back; if she were to hear I am prevented from getting home by illness, she would probably start off to join me, and she might quite possibly lose her reason on the road. She is getting old. I must make up some explanation of my delay, but it can only be a very short one. I can only give you a fortnight, either to bury me or set me on my legs again."

"Very good," quoth the doctor; "if you will make up your mind to obey my orders, you may travel in a fortnight."

He kept his word; on the fourteenth day I was out of the wood, and eight and forty hours after I had started for Leipzig, where Mendelssohn was living, with a letter of introduction to him from his sister, Madame Henzel.

Mendelssohn received me wonderfully—I use the expression advisedly, to describe the condescension extended by such an illustrious man to a youth who could not in his eyes have been more than a novice. I can truly say that for the four days I spent at Leipzig he devoted himself to me. He questioned me about my studies and my works with the keenest and sincerest interest. He made me play some of my later efforts to him, and gave me precious words of approbation and encouragement. One sentence only will I quote; I am too proud of it ever to have forgotten it. I had just played him the "Dies Iræ" from my Vienna Requiem. He laid his finger on a passage written for five voices without accompaniment, and said—

"My boy, that might have been written by Cherubini!"

Such words from such a master are better than any decoration—more precious to their recipient than all the ribbons and stars in Europe.

Mendelssohn was Director of the "Gewandhaus" Philharmonic Society. As the concert season was over, there were no meetings of the society going on, but he showed me the delicate kindness of calling its members together for my benefit. Thus I heard his beautiful work known as the "Scotch Symphony" in A Minor, and he afterwards gave me the full score endorsed with a few kind words in his own handwriting.

Too soon, alas! the early death of that splendid genius, in the heyday of his beauty and his charm, was to transform this friendly memento into a treasured and precious relic. He died only six months after the charming woman to whom I owed my acquaintance with her gifted brother.

Mendelssohn did not confine himself to calling the Philharmonic Society together for my benefit. An admirable organist himself, he was anxious I should make acquaintance with some of the numerous and admirable works composed by the mighty Sebastian Bach for the instrument over which he reigned supreme. With this object, he had the old organ at St. Thomas's—the very instrument Bach himself used—examined and repaired, and there for two long hours and more he revealed an unknown world of beauty to my wondering ears.

Finally, to crown it all, he presented me with a collection of motets by this same Bach, who was a sort of god to him, in whose school he had been formed from infancy, and whose Passion music, "according to St. Matthew," he had conducted and accompanied by heart before he was fifteen.

Such was the kind treatment I received at the hands of that most lovable of men, that splendid artist, that magnificent musician, cut off, alas! in the flower of his age (just eight-and-thirty), snatched from the plaudits he had earned so well, and from the yet more glorious results the later efforts of his talent might have yielded. Strange is the fate of genius, even when endued with the charm possessed by his! It was not till Mendelssohn himself was dead that the ears which would not hearken in his lifetime learnt to appreciate the exquisite works which are now the joy and delight of every subscriber to the Conservatoire concerts.

Once I had seen Mendelssohn I could think of nothing except of getting back as fast as possible to Paris and to my beloved mother. I left Leipzig on May 18, 1843. I changed carriages seventeen times on the road, and travelled four nights out of six. At length, on May 25, I reached Paris, where my life was to enter on a new and different phase. I found my brother waiting for me when the mail-coach arrived, and together we hurried to that beloved home into which I was about to carry so much new happiness, and return to so much that I had left behind.

IV
HOME AGAIN

WHETHER my three and a half years of absence had wrought a mighty change in my appearance, or my last illness (still very recent) and the stains of travel had played havoc with my looks, I know not, but anyhow my mother did not recognise me when I arrived. True, I had a budding beard, but such a slight one, that any one might have counted every hair.

During my absence my mother had left the Rue de l'Éperon, and settled down in the Rue Vaneau, in the parish known as "Les Missions Etrangères," the church of which stands at the corner of the Rue du Bac and the Rue de Babylone. There a post awaited me which was to fill up my time for several years to come. The priest of this parish, the Abbé Dumarsais, had formerly been chaplain at the Lycée St. Louis. His predecessor at the Missions Etrangères was the Abbé Lecourtier.

While I was in Rome at the Académie de France, the Abbé Dumarsais had written to offer me, on my return, the appointment of organist and chapel-master to his parish. This I had accepted, but under certain conditions. I had no notion of taking any advice, and still less any orders, on musical matters, from priest or parish authorities, or anybody else. I had my own ideas, my own opinions, my own convictions. In short, I meant either to have my own way about the music, or not have anything to do with it. That was flat. However, my conditions were accepted, and all should have gone smoothly.

But old habit is hard to break. My predecessor had accustomed the worthy parishioners to a style of music quite different from that which I had brought back with me from Rome and Germany. Palestrina and Bach were deities in *my* eyes, and I was casting down the idols *they* were accustomed to worship.

The means at my disposal were almost *nil*. Besides the organ—a small and very inferior instrument—I had two basses, a tenor, and one choir-boy, without reckoning myself, who was chapel-master, organist, singer, and composer all in one. I had to do my best with what I found to my hand, and the necessity which forced me to use these very modest resources to the best possible advantage was of real benefit to me in the long run. Things went on well enough at first, but I guessed, from a sort of coldness and reserve I noticed, that I was not altogether in the good books of the congregation. I was not mistaken. About the end of my first year of office, the priest sent for me, and confided to me that he had to endure many complaints and reproaches from his flock. Monsieur or Madame So-and-so did not consider the musical part of the service the least bit cheerful or entertaining. He therefore suggested to me to "change my style," and to "give in to them a little."

"My dear Abbé," I said, "you know our bargain. I didn't come here to consult the taste of your parishioners, but to improve it. If they don't like my 'style,' as you call it, there is a simple way out of the difficulty. I will resign, you can reappoint my predecessor, and everybody will be satisfied. The matter is entirely in your own hands."

"Very well," said the Abbé; "all right. I accept your resignation."

Thereupon we parted the best of friends. I had not been home for more than half an hour when the Abbé's servant knocked at my door.

"Well, Jean, what is it?"

"Sir, Monsieur Abbé would like to see you."

"Oh, really! All right, Jean; say I will come in a moment."

When I met the Abbé he began again on the same subject.

"Come, come, my dear boy, it is a word and a blow with you really and truly! Is there no middle course? Do let us consider the matter calmly. You went off like a sky-rocket this morning!"

"My dear Abbé, there is not the slightest use in beginning it all over again. I stick to everything I have said. If I am to notice the objections of this person or that, I may just as well give up trying to do anything at all. Either I stay with a perfectly free hand, or else I go. Those are my conditions, as you know, and I will not alter them one jot."

"Oh dear! oh dear!" he said, "what a terrible fellow you are!" And then after a pause, "Well then, you had better stop!"

From that day forth he never mentioned the subject again, and left me absolute liberty of action. Little by little, my bitterest opponents became my warmest supporters, and the increasing sympathy of my hearers soon caused my modest salary to swell. I had begun with 1200 francs a year, which was not a large sum. The second year my pay was increased by 300 francs; the third I had 1800, and the fourth 2100 francs. But I must not anticipate.

We lived, my mother and I, in the same house as the Abbé. Another priest, three years older than myself, who had been a schoolfellow of mine at the Lycée St. Louis, resided under the same roof—the Abbé Charles Gay. In the ordinary course of events, the disparity of our ages and his seniority in the school would have prevented any intimacy between us, even if we had happened to be acquainted with each other. However, our common taste for music had brought us together at the Lycée. Charles Gay, who was then about fourteen, had very remarkable musical aptitude, and used to take the second soprano parts in the choruses; he was also one of the most brilliant scholars at the college. He concluded his studies, and I lost sight of him for three years. I met him again in the Foyer at the Opera one night, when "La Juive" was being played. I knew him at once, and accosted him.

"Hallo!" he said, "is that you? And what are you doing with yourself?"

"I have gone in for composing."

"Really!" he said. "So have I. Who are you working with?"

"With Reicha."

"Why, so am I. This is delightful; we must see a lot of each other!"

Thus it was that our schoolboy friendship was renewed, and still remains one of the strongest of my life.

I had the greatest admiration for my friend, who possessed musical powers of the very highest order, and whose talent, as I freely recognised, far surpassed my own. His compositions struck me as being full of genius, and I envied him the career I felt sure the future had in store for him. I often spent my evenings in his rooms, where there was always plenty of music going on. His sister was an excellent pianiste, and besides his own compositions (which we often used to try over, among his intimate friends), trios by Mozart and Beethoven were frequently given.

One day I received a note from my friend (who was out of town) asking me to come and see him, as he had something interesting to tell me. My first thought was that he was going to be married; but when I reached his house, he told me he was anxious to enter the Church. This explained all the folios and other big books I had for some time remarked lying about on his table. I was too young then to grasp the meaning of so sudden a change, and I regretted his decision to sacrifice such a smiling future to a life which seemed to me devoid of charm.

Meanwhile he made up his mind to pay a visit to Rome, and there begin his theological studies. I myself had just won the Grand Prix, which necessitated my going to Rome for two years. So it fell out that I met my friend again, he having arrived some three months before myself. When I came back from Germany, luck brought us together again by settling us under the same roof.

The Abbé Gay has now been a priest for more than thirty years, and is the Vicar-General of his intimate friend the Bishop of Poitiers.[12] Not his virtues only, but his talents as a speaker and a writer too, have brought him the reputation of being one of the most eminent ornaments the French clergy boasts.

Towards the third year of my duties as chapel-master, I myself felt a certain leaning towards an ecclesiastical career. Besides my musical studies, I had dabbled somewhat in philosophy and theology, and had even attended the theological lectures at the seminary at St. Sulpice all through one winter, wearing the dress of an ecclesiastical student.

But I had utterly mistaken my own nature and my proper vocation. I felt, after a time, that existence without my art was quite impossible for me, so, casting off the garb which suited me so ill, I went back into the world again. To this youthful phase of mine, however, I owe a friendship which I make it a point of honour to record in this chronicle of my life history.

[12] Since writing the above the Abbé Gay has become Bishop of Poitiers himself.

During the summer of 1846 I was ordered, with the Abbés Dumarsais and Gay, to take sea baths at Trouville. One day I had a narrow escape from drowning, and so quickly did the press get hold of the fact, that the news was published next morning even in the Paris papers. Luckily I had lost no time in writing to tell my brother I was safe, so he was able to calm my mother's fears by showing her my letter. The papers had calmly announced that "I had been brought home dead on a shutter!" Truly the flimsiest truth travels slower than the weightiest lie! We chanced during this sea-bathing trip to come across a worthy Abbé walking on the beach with a boy, who was his pupil. This boy, some twelve or thirteen years of age, was named Gaston de Beaucourt. His mother, the Comtesse de Beaucourt, owned a fine property some leagues from Trouville, between Pont l'Evêque and Lisieux. She invited us, in the most courteous and kindly way, to go and stay there before returning to Paris.

That charming and lovable boy, now a man of three-and-forty, and one of the best that ever lived, became my lifelong friend, to whose affection, sure and strong and tender, I owe not only the happiness our perfect mutual comprehension brings, but many a precious proof of the deepest and most unselfish devotion.

The Revolution of 1848 had just broken out when I resigned my post as chapel-master of the Missions Etrangères. My duties during the four and a half years I held it had served me admirably in the development and improvement of my musical education; but they were not calculated to advance my career to any practical extent, for they kept me vegetating in a corner, as it were. There is only one road for a composer who desires to make a real name—the operatic stage. The stage is the one place where a musician can find constant opportunity and means of communicating with the public. It is a sort of daily and permanent exhibition where his works can be perpetually on view.

Religious and symphonic music no doubt rank higher, in the strictest sense, than dramatic composition; but opportunities for distinction in that highest sphere are very rare, and can only affect an occasional audience, not a regular and systematic one like the opera-going public. Then, again, look at the huge variety of subject which lies before the dramatic author! What scope for fancy, for invention! what endless plots!

The stage tempted me irresistibly. I was nearly thirty, and eager to try my fortune on the fresh field I dreamt of. But I had no libretto, and I knew nobody whom I could ask to write me one. Then I had to find an impresario willing to employ me and trust me with a commission; and who was likely to do that, in face of the undoubted fact that my previous training had been mostly confined to sacred music, and that I knew nothing about the stage? Altogether I was in a fix.

But fortune led me to a man who soon shed light upon my path. This was the violinist Seghers, who then managed the concerts of the Société Ste. Cecile, in the Rue de la Chaussée d'Antin. Some compositions of mine had been performed at these concerts, and very favourably received. Seghers was a friend of the Viardots. Madame Viardot was then at the zenith of her talent and reputation—this was in 1849, just when she had created the *rôle* of Fides in Meyerbeer's "Le Prophète" with such tremendous success. Madame Viardot received me with the utmost kindness, and suggested my letting her hear some of my work. I complied, of course, with the greatest delight. We spent a long time at the piano, and after listening to me with the kindest attention, she said—

"But, Monsieur Gounod, why do you not write an opera?"

"Indeed, Madame," I replied, "I would gladly do so, but I have no libretto."

"But surely you know somebody who could write you one?"

"Oh yes, no doubt I do; but 'could' and 'would' are very different words! I know, or rather when I was a child I *used* to know, Emile Augier; we trundled our hoops together in the Luxemburg. But since those days Augier has grown famous, and I have remained in my native obscurity. I hardly think my old playmate would care to join me in anything more risky than a hoop race!"

"Very well," said Madame Viardot, "go and see Augier, and tell him that if he will write the libretto I will sing the principal part in your opera."

My readers may fancy I did not wait to be told that twice. I tore off to Augier, who accepted my suggestion with enthusiastic delight.

"What! Madame Viardot!" he cried. "I should rather think so! I will set to work at once!"

Nestor Roqueplan was then impresario at the Opera. He was quite willing, on Madame Viardot's recommendation, to give up part of an evening's performance to my work, but he could not, he said, spare more. So we had to look for a subject which would combine three essential points—(1) brevity, (2) interest, (3) a central female figure. We pitched on the story of Sappho. The opera could not, in any case, be put into rehearsal till the following year; besides, Augier had to finish a big work he was then employed on. It was, I believe, his "Diane" for Mademoiselle Rachel.

At all events I held a formal promise, and I awaited the event with mingled impatience and calm. Just as I was about to set to work, a crushing blow fell on me and mine. This was in April 1850. Augier had just finished the poem of "Sappho." My brother was taken ill on the 2nd; on the 3rd I signed my agreement with Roqueplan, whereby I undertook to hand him over the score of "Sappho" by September 30 at latest. This allowed me six months to compose and write a three-act opera, my maiden dramatic effort. On the night of the 6th of April my brother breathed his last. It was a fearful grief to my old mother and to all of us.

My brother left a widow, with a child of two years old, and the prospect of another. It was born seven months later, opening its baby eyes on this sad world on the very day when the Church joins us in mourning the memory of our beloved dead.

These sad circumstances induced many difficulties and complications which demanded close and immediate attention. The guardianship of the children, the carrying on of my brother's business as an architect (for his death left much work still unfinished), every possible consequence, in fact, of such a sudden and unforeseen disaster, forced me to devote my time for quite a month to safeguarding the interests and arranging for the future of my unhappy sister-in-law, whose grief had quite prostrated her, physically and mentally. Besides all this, my poor mother nearly lost her reason under the stunning blow which had fallen on her. Every circumstance, both personal and external, seemed combined to unfit me utterly for an undertaking for which the time at my disposal already seemed so insufficient.

Within about a month, however, I was able to think seriously of making the beginning which was growing so urgently necessary. Madame Viardot, who had been on tour in Germany, and whom I had informed of the sad trouble we were in, wrote at once to urge me to take my mother with me and settle down for a while at a country place of her own in the neighbourhood of La Brie, where, she said, I should have the quiet and calm I needed.

I took her advice, and my mother and I started for Madame Viardot's house, where we found her mother (Madame Garcia, widow of the famous singer), a sister of Monsieur Viardot's and a girl, his eldest child, who is now Madame Heritte, and a composer of considerable note. There, too, I met a most delightful man, Ivan Tourgueneff, the celebrated Russian author, a close and intimate friend of the Viardot family.

I set to work at once. Though—strange fact!—the feelings which had been so lately torn by painful emotion might naturally have been expected to find their first expression in sorrow-laden and pathetic strains, just the reverse took place. The first ideas that came to me were full of gaiety and brightness, and they filled all my brain, as if my inner nature, crushed down by grief and mourning, felt the need of some reaction, and longed to draw a breath of happier life after my long hours of anguish and days of tears and bitter mourning.

Thanks to the calmness of the atmosphere around me, my work progressed much faster than I had dared to hope. After her German tour, Madame Viardot's engagements took her to England, whence she returned in the beginning of September, and found my labour nearly completed. I hastened to play her my work, of which I anxiously desired her opinion. She was quite satisfied with it, and in the course of a few days she knew the score so well, that she was able to accompany the whole of it by heart. This is about the most wonderful musical feat I ever witnessed, and gives some idea of the extraordinary powers of that splendid musician.

"Sappho" was performed for the first time on April 16, 1851, just before my thirty-second birthday. It was not a success, but, all the same, it earned me a good position in the opinion of contemporary artists. It does indeed betray a lack of theatrical instinct, a want of knowledge of stage effect, and of the resources of an orchestra, and some ignorance in handling it. But, on the other hand, the expression is true in feeling, the appreciation of the subject, from the lyrical point of view, is fairly exact, and the general style of treatment is distinctly dignified in tendency. The finale of the first act produced an effect which fairly astonished me. It was loudly and unanimously encored. I could hardly believe my ears, though they were tingling with the unaccustomed emotion, but the encore was repeated at every subsequent performance.

The effect of the second act was not so good as that of the first, in spite of the success of an air sung by Madame Viardot, and of the light duet, "Va m'attendre, mon maître," sung by Brémond and Mdlle. Poinsot. But the third act made a very good impression. The goatherd's song, "Broutez le thym, broutez mes chèvres," was encored, and Sappho's final stanza, "O ma lyre immortelle," were loudly applauded.

The cowherd's song gave the tenor Aymès his first opportunity of appearing in public; he sang it beautifully, and thereby laid the foundation of his reputation. Gueymard and Marié took the parts of Phaon and Alcée.

My mother was present, of course, at the first performance of my opera. As I passed along one of the corridors on the way from the stage to the auditorium, where I was to meet her after the crowd had dispersed, I came upon my friend Berlioz, his eyes still wet with tears. I threw my arm round him, and said—

"Oh, dear Berlioz, come and show those wet eyes of yours to my mother. No newspaper paragraph about my opera will make her half so proud."

He granted my request, and said to her—

"Madame, I do not think anything has touched me so much for the last twenty years."

He afterwards published a notice of my opera, which I still regard as one of the most flattering and precious I have ever had the delight and honour of receiving.

"Sappho" was only acted six times. Madame Viardot's engagement was almost over, and her place in the opera was taken by Mdlle. Masson, who only sang the part three times.

I think it may safely be laid down as a general principle, that a theatrical work always, or almost always, has the public reception it really deserves. Theatrical success so inevitably depends on a variety of small details, that the failure of any one—of the merest accessories even—may (as has frequently happened) counterbalance, and perhaps utterly compromise, the effect of the finest qualities of conception and performance. Staging, ballet, scenery, dresses, book, fifty things go to make or mar an opera. The public, if its interest is to be kept alive, demands constant "variety." Many works of the very highest merit in some respects, have failed, not in rousing the admiration of true artists, but in winning popular favour, simply through their lack of this "spice," so indispensable to that class of the public which is not content with the simple charm of intellectual beauty.

I do not for a moment desire to claim the benefit of this excuse for my "Sappho." The public's right of passing judgment on any work offered to it is based on a prerogative peculiar to itself, and conferring special competence. It would be unfair to ask or expect it to possess that specific knowledge which would enable it to decide as to the technical value of a work of art. But, on the other hand, the public has a distinct right to expect and demand that a play or opera should satisfy those particular instincts the satisfaction and gratification of which it seeks within the playhouse walls. The success of a dramatic work then does not depend solely on the quality of its form and style. Both are no doubt essential—nay, indispensable—to save it from the rapid ravages of Time, whose scythe spares naught that is not essentially true and beautiful. But form and style are not its only, nor even, in a sense, its strongest support. They may and do strengthen and solidify success; they cannot make it.

The theatre-going public is a sort of dynamometer. It has nothing to do with the question of whether the play is in good taste or not. Its sole duty is to gauge what constitutes the true essence of every dramatic work—the strength of passion and the degree of emotion it expresses; its rendering, in fact, of the feelings which sway all human souls, individually and collectively. The consequence is, that author and audience become unconscious instruments in their mutual artistic education. The public is the author's criterion and measure of truth; the author serves his public as an exhibitor of the elements and conditions of the beautiful. This explanation is the only one, to my mind, which can account for the mysterious and incessant changes in public taste. What was madly sought for yesterday is neglected to-day; one evening will see men ready to tear to pieces the very thing the next morning will see them worshipping on bended knees.

Though not exactly a success, "Sappho" brought me some solid advantage, both present and future. On the very night of the first performance, Ponsard asked me to undertake the choral music for "Ulysse," a tragedy in five acts which he was just bringing out at the Théâtre Français. I agreed at once, although I did not know the play. It was quite enough for me to have the chance of collaborating with the author of "Lucrece," of "Charlotte Corday," and of "Agnès de Méranie." I felt quite safe. Arsène Houssaye was then at the head of the Comédie Française. He was obliged to add a chorus to the ordinary staff, and increase the orchestra as well.[13]

"Ulysse" was played on June 18, 1852. I had been married a few days previously to a daughter of Zimmerman,[14] the distinguished Professor of the Piano at the Conservatoire. To his school we owe Prudent, Marmontel, Goria, Lefebure-Wély, Ravina, Bizet, and many other fine musicians. By this marriage I became brother-in-law to the young painter, Edouard Dubufe, who was even then successfully following in his father's footsteps. His son, Guillaume Dubufe, seems, at the time I write, to be likely to maintain the reputation of his forefathers right worthily.

The principal parts in "Ulysse" were filled by Mademoiselle Judith, Messieurs Geffroy, Delaunay, and Maubant, Mademoiselle Nathalie, and others. The musical portion of the performance consisted of no less than fourteen choruses, one tenor solo, several melodramatic instrumental passages, and an orchestral overture. There was a certain risk of monotony in the general effect, as the composer was limited to orchestra and chorus; but I was fortunate enough to avoid the difficulty fairly well, and this second work of mine earned me fresh good-will in the artistic world. No publisher had offered to publish the score of "Sappho," but that of "Ulysse" was more favoured. Messieurs Escudier did me the honour and the kindness of printing it free of charge.

"Ulysse" had a run of forty performances. It was the second ordeal, as regards

[13] See letter from Berlioz to Gounod, dated November 19, 1851.

[14] See letter from Gounod to Lefuel, undated.

dramatic composition, through which my mother had watched me pass. The choruses of "Ulysse," as far as I can judge them, are fairly correct in character and expression, and are marked by a distinctly personal style. The orchestral treatment still fails from lack of experience, more than in actual colour, the general feeling for which strikes me as being fairly good.

A few days after my marriage I was appointed Superintendent of Instruction in Singing to the Communal Schools of the City of Paris, and Director of the Choral Society connected with them, in the place of Monsieur Hubert, himself the pupil and successor of Wilhem, the original creator of the said society.

This post I held for eight years and a half, and its duties were of the greatest service to me, musically speaking. They taught me to direct and utilise large masses of vocal sound, so as to develop the maxim of sonority under very simple methods of treatment.

My third musical venture on the stage was "La Nonne Sanglante," an opera in five acts, by Scribe and Germain Delarigne. Nestor Roqueplan, who was still Director of the Opera, had taken a fancy to "Sappho" and to me. I was capable, so he declared, of doing great things, and at his wish I wrote a five-act piece for the Opera. "La Nonne Sanglante" was written in 1852-53, rehearsed for the first time on October 18, 1853, put aside and rehearsed again several times over, and finally saw the footlights on October, 18, 1854, just a year after the first rehearsal. It was only acted eight times. Roqueplan was succeeded as Director of the Opera by Monsieur Crosnier, and as the new chief declared he would not allow "such stuff" to be acted, "La Nonne Sanglante" disappeared from the bills, and has never shown her face again.

It was rather a grief to me. The very respectable figure reached by the receipts certainly did not warrant such drastic and summary treatment. But directorial decisions sometimes, so I have heard it whispered, have hidden motives which it is vain to try and discover. In such cases the real reason is concealed, and some other pretext put forward.

I cannot say whether "La Nonne Sanglante" would have had any permanent success—I am inclined to think not. Not that the work was poor in effects; there were some most striking situations. But the subject is too uniformly gloomy. It had the drawback, too, of having a plot that was more than fanciful or improbable; it was downright impossible, and depended on a purely imaginary situation, utterly false, and therefore devoid of dramatic interest, which cannot exist without truthfulness, or at all events something approaching thereto.

I think, in the matter of orchestration, I made a forward stride in "La Nonne Sanglante." Some parts show an increased knowledge of instrumentation, and seem to bear the impress of a firmer hand. There is good colour in many scenes—such, for instance, as the Crusaders' Hymn, with Peter the Hermit and the chorus, in the first act; the symphonic prelude in the ruins, and the Ghosts' March, in the second; the tenor air and the duet with the Nun, in the third.

The principal parts were played by Mesdemoiselles Wertheimber and Poinsot, and Messieurs Gueymard, Depassio, and Merly.

I solaced my disappointment by writing a symphony (No. 1 in D) for the Société des Jeunes Artistes, which had just been started by Pasdeloup, and which held its concerts in the Salle Herz, in the Rue de la Victoire. This symphony was so well received that I wrote another (No. 2 in E flat) for the same society. It too achieved a certain success.

About the same time I composed a Solemn Mass for St. Cecilia's Day, which was successfully performed for the first time on November 22, 1855, by the Association des Artistes Musiciens, in the Church of St. Eustache, and has often been given since. I dedicated this Mass to the memory of my father-in-law Zimmerman, whom we had lost on October 29, 1853.

Yet another misfortune overtook our family; on August 6, 1855, death snatched away my wife's elder sister, Juliette Dubufe, wife of Edouard Dubufe the painter, a rare and gifted creature, full of charming qualities, and of exceptional talent as a sculptress and a pianiste. "Goodness, wit, talent"—these are the words inscribed upon her tomb; a simple epitaph, but eloquent in its simplicity and well deserved, fitly expressing as it does the honour and regret showered on the memory of an exquisite nature, the charm of which fell irresistibly on all who approached her.

Nearly all my time was taken up with the management of the Choral Society. I wrote a number of things for the big concerts of this institution. Some were very well received; among others two Masses, one of which had been performed under my direction on June 12, 1853, at the Church of St Germain l'Auxerrois in Paris. During one of these great annual meetings of the Choral Society, on Sunday, June 8, 1856, my wife presented me with a son. (Three years before, on the 13th of the same month, we had mourned the loss of our eldest child, a girl, who was born dead). On the morning of the day when my boy was born, my brave wife contrived to hide her sufferings from me until I left home for the concert; and on my return in the afternoon, I found my son had opened his eyes upon the world.

The birth of this child, which I had deeply longed for, was a joy and a blessing to us both. He has been mercifully spared to us, is now over one-and-twenty, and hopes to be a painter.

Since the withdrawal of "La Nonne Sanglante" I had done no dramatic work; but I had written a short oratorio, called "Tobie," which George Hainl (then conductor of the orchestra at the Grand Théâtre at Lyons) had asked me to compose for one of his annual benefit concerts. This oratorio, as it strikes me, has certain qualities both of sentiment and of expression. Some attention was attracted by a somewhat touching air for the youthful Tobias, and by several other passages which had a good deal of pathos about them. In 1856 I made the acquaintance of Jules Barbier and Michel Carré. I suggested to them to collaborate with me, and trust me with a libretto. They agreed to do so in a very friendly way. The first subject I put forward for collaboration was "Faust." The idea pleased them both. We went to see Monsieur Carvalho, at that time Director of the Théâtre Lyrique, in the Boulevard du Temple. He had just brought out Victor Massé's "Reine Topaze," in which Madame Miolan-Carvalho had achieved a striking success. Monsieur Carvalho approved of our notion, and my two friends set to work at once. I had myself done about half my share of the work, when Monsieur Carvalho suddenly informed me that the Théâtre de la Porte Saint Martin was on the point of bringing out a melodrama under the name of "Faust," and that this fact completely upset his calculations with regard to our work. He rightly thought we should never be ready before the Porte Saint Martin, and even so, it would be imprudent to enter into competition with a theatre whose well-known splendour as to *mise en scène* would draw half Paris just before our piece appeared.

He therefore begged us to choose some other subject, but this sudden upset made it impossible for me to turn my thoughts into another channel, and for more than a week I was unable to do any work at all.

At last Monsieur Carvalho asked me to write a comic opera, and to take my subject from Molière. This was the origin of the "Médecin malgré lui," which was produced at the Théâtre Lyrique on January 15, 1858, the anniversary of Molière's birth.

The announcement of a comic opera from the pen of a musician whose former ventures had been in such a different style seemed to bode disappointment. But these fears (some of them were hopes perhaps?) were not justified by the event, for the "Médecin malgré lui" was, *malgré cela,* my first really successful opera.[15]

But all my delight was shattered by the death of my poor mother. She had been ill for some months, and completely blind for two years previously. She died on January 16, 1858, the very day after the first performance, aged seventy-seven years and a half. Fate did not permit me to brighten her last days with the fruit of my labour, and the just recompense of the life she had so unceasingly devoted to her children and their future. I can only hope that before she left us she knew and foresaw that her struggle had not been in vain, and that her self-sacrifice had brought a great reward.

The "Médecin malgré lui" had an uninterrupted run of a hundred nights. The work was staged with the greatest care. Monsieur Got, of the Comédie Française, was good enough, at the request of the Director, to bestow his invaluable advice as to the traditional mounting of the piece and the declamation of the spoken dialogue. The chief part, that of Sganarelle, was played by the baritone Meillet, whose voice was full and round, and his play spirited. He made a great success both as a singer and an actor. The other male parts were taken by Girardot, Wartel, Fromant, and Lesage (the two latter afterwards replaced by Potel and Gabriel), and all in the very best manner. The two principal ladies' parts were held by Mesdemoiselles Faivre and Girard, both of them full of life and animation.

This score, the first comic work I ever did, is in a light and easy style which savours of the Italian opera-bouffe. I have endeavoured to recall the style of Lulli in certain passages, but the work as a whole keeps to the modern forms, and belongs to the French school. Among the numbers which most took the public taste were the "Chanson des Glouglous," excellently sung by Meillet, and invariably encored; the "Trio de la Bastonnade," the "Sextuor de la Consultation," a "Fabliau," the "Scène de Consultation des Paysans," and a duet for Sganarelle and the

[15] See letter from Gounod to one of his brothers-in-law, Monsieur Pigny.

nurse.

The Porte-Saint-Martin "Faust" had just been brought out; but all its magnificent staging did not ensure the melodrama a very long run. Monsieur Carvalho consequently reverted to our former plan, and I at once set to work upon the opera which I had laid aside to write the "Médecin."

My "Faust" was first put into rehearsal in September 1858. Before I left Paris for Switzerland, where I was to spend the holidays with my wife and son, then two years old, I had gone through the work with Monsieur Carvalho in the Foyer of his theatre. At that time nothing had been settled as to the cast, and Monsieur Carvalho had asked my leave to bring his wife, who lived opposite the theatre, to hear me play over the work. She was so struck with the *rôle* of Marguerite, that Monsieur Carvalho begged me to let her sing it. I was naturally only too delighted, and the result proved my decision to have been something like an inspiration.

All the same, the rehearsals of "Faust" were not fated to pursue "the even tenor of their way" without many checks and difficulties. The tenor who was to have played "Faust," although gifted with a beautiful voice and a handsome presence, turned out not to be equal to so heavy a part. A short time before the date fixed for the first performance, it became necessary to find some one to take his place; and the part was offered to Monsieur Barbot, who happened to be disengaged. Within a month Barbot had mastered it and was ready to perform. So the opera was acted for the first time on March 19, 1859.

Though "Faust" did not strike the public very much at first, it is the greatest theatrical success I have ever had. Do I mean that it is the best thing I have written? That I cannot tell. I can only reiterate the opinion I have already expressed, that success is more the result of a certain concatenation of favourable elements and successful conditions, than a proof and criterion of the intrinsic value of a work. Public favour is attracted in the first instance by outward appearances; all inward and solid qualities can do is to retain and strengthen it. It takes some time to grasp and absorb the innumerable details which go to make up a drama.

Dramatic art is a branch of the art of portraiture; its function is to delineate character, as that of the painter is to present feature and attitude. Every lineament, all those momentary and fleeting inflections which constitute that individual physiognomy known as a "personality," must be grasped and reproduced. Shakespeare's immortal figures of Hamlet, Richard III., Othello, and Lady Macbeth are so true to the type which each expresses, that they hold a real and living place in every mind. Well may they be called "creations."

Dramatic music is ruled by the same laws, and cannot otherwise exist. Its object, too, is to portray feature; but where painting conveys an impression at a glance, music has to tell its story by degrees, and thus often fails to produce the intended effect at a first hearing.

None of my previous works could have led the world to expect anything like "Faust" from me; it was a surprise to the public, both as to style and interpretation.

Of course the part of Marguerite was not the first in which Madame Carvalho had found scope for that marvellous style and power of execution which have set her in the highest place among contemporary singers; but no previous *rôle* had given her so fine an opportunity of displaying the lyric and pathetic side of her gifts. Her Marguerite made her reputation in this respect, and will always be one of the glories of her brilliant career. Barbot sang the difficult part of Faust like the great musician he is. Balanqué, who created the part of Mephistopheles, was a clever actor, whose gesture, appearance, and voice admirably suited that weird and diabolical personage. Although he somewhat overacted the part, he made a great success. The smaller parts of Siebel and Valentine were very creditably performed by Mademoiselle Faivre and Monsieur Raynal.

As to the score itself, it raised such a whirlwind of debate and criticism, that my hopes of a real success grew faint indeed.

LETTERS

I

Monsieur H. Lefuel, *Poste Restante, Genoa.*

(If Monsieur Lefuel does not call for his letters at Genoa, kindly forward to the Académie de France at Rome.)

Vienna, *Monday, August 21, 1842.*

My dear Hector,—Some week or so ago I had a letter from Hébert, to whom I had written in the first instance from Vienna. He tells me you are somewhere near Genoa, but cannot exactly tell me where. As you have consistently neglected me, my dear fellow, all through my travels, and as I found no news of you at either Florence, Venice, or Vienna, I was obliged to ask a mutual friend whether he happened to know your address and could let me have it. From Hébert's answer I gather he has been luckier than I. He knew your whereabouts at anyrate, and could write to you, and get news of you. Yet you were perfectly well aware, hateful old monster that you are, that your sorrowing relation would have rejoiced over even the veriest line from you. But not a scratch of your pen have I seen all through my journey. So how was I to write to you? I longed to always, and you never gave me a chance of doing it! As likely as not, this letter will arrive and find you flown, which accounts for the extreme precautions you may observe in the directions on my envelope.

If I were anywhere within reach, I should have a real good row with you. What on earth are you thinking of? Has your patriarchal tenderness waxed so faint that you feel no temptation to write your eldest-born a few of those inspiring sentences he so deeply values? Even supposing you had not had time to write, I might at all events have kept you posted about many matters which interested me then, and do so still, and which would not have been indifferent, I think, to you.

However, now I have had my grumble, dearest and best of friends and patriarchs, I will forget your crimes, and grant you my hearty pardon. I know right well how you detest all letter-writing; I know, too, that you never waste your time. That fact was made so clear to me at Rome, that I never dreamt of putting down your silence to laziness. So I will forget everything, except our mutual friendship.

I have wanted for some time to let you hear of a bit of good fortune I have had here. The Mass I wrote in Rome, for the King's fête-day at San Luigi de Francesi, is to be performed, with full orchestra, here in Vienna, on the 6th of September. This is a piece of luck which has never fallen in the way of any other Academy student, and has only come in mine through my having made acquaintance with some kindly artists, who have introduced me to others who have special influence here.

I am working very hard; I see very few people, and seldom go out. I am up to the eyes in a Requiem with full orchestral accompaniment, which will probably be performed in Germany on November 2. The officials of the church where my Roman Mass is to be given have already offered to have my Requiem done as well. But as I am not yet quite certain whether I shall think the rendering of the Mass satisfactory, I give no decided answer for the present. Through my acquaintance with Madame Henzel and with Mendelssohn, I might be able to secure a far finer performance of the work in Berlin, and this would have the advantage of raising me much higher in the opinion of my brother artists. But my hands are still quite free as regards the Vienna performance. If I am satisfied with the way my Mass is given on September 8, I shall let them do the Requiem here; if not, I shall take it to Berlin. When Madame Henzel was in Rome, she said to me, "When you come to Germany, my brother might be of the greatest use to you, if you have any music you wish to have performed."

I wrote to her to Berlin some days ago, and as I mean to leave this on September 12, and make a tour through Munich, Leipzig, Berlin, Dresden, and Prague, I asked her to be good enough to tell me if she thought I might hope to get any of my music performed in Berlin. When I get her answer, I shall see my way clearer. If she says yes, I shall stop in Berlin until the beginning of November, and then go straight back to Paris; if she says no, I shall return to Vienna, to which place the railway would get me back in four days. There is a line from Vienna to Olmutz, which would save me about sixty leagues. If I have to stop in Berlin for my Requiem, I shall travel by a different route; thus, Munich, Prague, Dresden, and Leipzig to Berlin. In any case I will let you know, as soon as I know myself.

I often regret our beautiful Rome, my dear Hector, and cordially do I envy those who have the luck to be there still. I really think my recollection of that lovely land is the chief charm and happiness of my present life. If you only *knew* what all the other countries I have travelled through look like after Italy!

The last thing I saw, and it made a deep and lasting impression on me, was Venice. You know all its beauties, so I will not go into long descriptions or ecstasies of admiration. You know all my feelings on the subject.

No doubt, dear friend, you have heard of the death of our comrade Blanchard. Deeply as I regret him, I know your grief is greater still, for you knew him far better even than I did. Such shadows are well-nigh sure to fall on every meeting after prolonged separation, and, commonplace as it may sound, there is something terribly indispensable about that word which closes every letter one writes.

Farewell, dear friend, farewell! I greet you as friend greets friend, nay, more, as brother greets brother. I hope *we,* at least, may meet again! Good-bye.—Ever yours,

CHARLES GOUNOD.

II

Monsieur Charles Gounod,
47 Rue Pigalle, Paris.

November 19.

My dear Gounod,—I have just gone through your choruses for "Ulysse" with the greatest care. The work as a whole seems to me to have considerable merit, and the interest of the music rises as that of the drama intensifies. The double chorus of "the Banquet" is exceedingly good, and will make a powerful effect if properly performed. I do not think the Comédie Française can or will be at all stingy in the matter of your orchestra. The music alone, to my mind, will suffice to draw the public for a considerable number of nights, and it should therefore be to the direct and pecuniary interest of the Director that a large proportion of what is laid out on producing the play should be allocated to the musical part of the work. I think this will turn out to be the case. At the same time, do not give an inch on the matter. Get what you want, or take nothing at all. Be very careful who you give your solos to; one bad singer will utterly spoil the chances of a whole song.

Look at the page I have turned down; there is a mistake in the time, just at the opening of a verse, which I think you would be wise to alter. Men like you and me oughtn't to scan like that. We must leave that sort of thing to people who don't know their work. Best and sincerest good wishes.—Yours always,

H. Berlioz.

III

Monsieur Hector Lefuel,
20 Rue du Tournon, Paris.

My dear Hector,—I called on you about a month ago to tell you a very important piece of news, which you, in your well-earned quality of friend and "father," have a right to know before anybody else. I am to be married next month to Mademoiselle Agnes Zimmerman. We are all as pleased as we can be, and I believe we may look forward to very solid and lasting happiness. My future wife's family is very good and kind, and I am lucky enough to be a general favourite there already.

I know, dear friend, you will be the first to congratulate me on this new and happy prospect. But our joy must be tinged with sadness when we think of the memories it must bring back to our poor Marthe[16], who still mourns the love she prized so much and lost so soon. God grant the sisterly affection my wife will give her may atone for the pangs the sight of our new-found happiness may cause her! I feel quite sure I may hope for this, for their two sweet natures are strongly drawn to each other even now.

Good-bye, dear Hector. Always yours most affectionately. My best regards to Madame Lefuel.

Charles Gounod.

[16] His widowed sister-in-law.

IV

Monsieur Pigny[17],
Rue d'Enghien, Paris.

Lucerne, *Tuesday, August 28, 1855.*

My dear Friend Pigny,—In my mother's letter, received to-day, she speaks with deep and grateful emotion of your more than filial devotion to her since my departure, and of the kindly care with which you offered to see personally to all the details of her move from the country. It is a considerable undertaking for an old lady like her, in spite of her simple wants and habits.

You who worship two mothers, so they tell me—self-sacrifice and renunciation (I use these names advisedly; I can find no other epithets to express my meaning)—will understand me when I tell you that what you do for her is the very tenderest and best thing you can do for me, for you help and complete a work I can never accomplish to my fullest satisfaction—I mean the endeavour to repay a tithe of the care, the sacrifices, the anxiety, the devotion she has lavished on me through many years of noble, patient, faithful toil. We have filled all her life, in fact, and she, alas! can only fill a part of ours.

I assure you, dear Pigny, I am most deeply touched by this proof that you already treat me as your friend. Apart from the universal affection in which all here hold you, nothing could give you greater claim and title to mine than the delicate deference and kindness you have so gracefully shown my honoured and beloved mother.

Charles Gounod.

---

[17] An architect, who had married another daughter of Zimmerman's.

LATER LETTERS OF CHARLES GOUNOD 1870-1871 [18]

I

VARANGEVILLE, *Sunday, September 4.*

MY DEARS,—As you may well imagine, our dear grandmother is very uncertain as to what she should do. You know kind Louisa Brown has written pressingly and repeatedly to offer grandmamma a home at Blackheath until she can settle down, and the invitation is specifically extended to *you* as well as to *ourselves*.

My own responsibility weighs heavy on me at this juncture. Persuasion or dissuasion strike me as being equally serious in their results. I should like to know dear Pigny's mind on the subject. As to my own ideas, here they are.

If cruel fortune gives Prussia the victory (no easy matter, as it seems to me), and if France is to be humiliated under a foreign conqueror, I should never have courage, I confess, to go on living under the enemy's yoke.

Well, granting the Emperor's captivity, MacMahon's defeat, and our loss of eighty thousand men to be undoubted and accomplished facts, my first duty, as it strikes me, is to convey our mother, my wife, and my two children to London, as a *provisional arrangement*. Speak, then, good Pigny! I hearken with all my ears!

II

8 MORDEN ROAD, BLACKHEATH, LONDON.

Yes, my dear fellow, you are perfectly right! The peace proposals Prussia dreams of are a crying shame. But the shame, thank God, lies wholly with the proposing party. They bring glory to those who reject them.

Like you I feel, I will not say humiliated, but cut to the very heart by the horrible misfortunes which have befallen our poor unhappy France. So much so, that I keep wondering, every hour of the day, whether the duty of those who are called to the honour and happiness of defending our country is not less heavy than that you and I have to perform, and which no man would choose if he felt he must blush for the performance of it. Alas! dear friend, this once, at all events, in history, Frenchmen in general have spilt their noble blood so gallantly, that the shame of

[18] With the exception of the fifth and eighth, which are addressed to Edouard Dubufe, these letters were written to Monsieur and Madame Pigny. The reader is doubtless aware that Pigny the architect, Dubufe the painter, and Gounod, married three daughters of Zimmerman the musical composer.

those who only think of their own personal safety clings to themselves alone. But the glory of victory nowadays (for the first time, perhaps, in this world's history) is won by machinery rather than by men, and disasters will be weighed in the same balance. The Prussians have not been braver than we. We have been less fortunate than they.

You know already, and I say it again, if you decide to re-enter any gate of Paris, I will not let you go alone. Family life means something more than mere family dinner!

Well, here we are at last, dear friend, in our new dwelling, after eighteen days spent in the enjoyment of the simplest and sincerest hospitality. Some Englishmen there are who will not let us Frenchmen feel we are in England. The manner in which our good and kind friend Brown has shared our trouble proves it.

But the external peace we have found here gives us no inward calm. The longer this horrible bloody war of pride and extermination lasts, the more do I feel my very heart-strings wrung with grief for my unhappy country; and anything that seems to rouse me from my sad contemplation of our beloved France, far from comforting me, as with kindness, stings like an insult.

Oh, most unhappy earth! wretched home of the human race! where barbarism not only still exists, but is taken for glory, and permitted to obscure the pure and beneficent rays of the only true glory in existence, the glory of love, of science, and of genius! Humanity yet lingers, it would seem, under the grim shadows of chaos, amidst the monstrosities of the iron age; and instead of driving their weapons into the earth to benefit their fellow-creatures, men plunge them into each other's hearts to decide the ownership of the actual soil. Barbarians! savages!

Ah, dear fellow, let me make an end, or I shall go on for ever, for very sorrow!

The dear ones near me, who are dear to you too, are well. Would we could have hidden them a little less far off—in Paris!

III

8 Morden Road, Blackheath Park, London,
Wednesday, October 12, 1870.

Dear Friends,—As our correspondence is the only thing we have left to help us struggle against the pain of separation, we ought, so far as circumstances permit, to make the most of it; for we cannot be sure, alas! that what can be done to-day will be possible to-morrow. So we have settled with grandmamma that we will write in turn, as long as you are at Varangeville. My turn falls to-day.

I have just seen a French newspaper, dear Pi, which reports that the Sous-Préfet of Dieppe has posted an order forbidding any Frenchman under sixty years of age to leave the country. So that you are now interned in France, not by your own will only, but by order of the authorities. But as I am not in France, and as I left before any such prohibition was published, I should like you to let me know whether this order is accompanied by another, which seems to me its inevitable corollary, or rather its cause, and its logical explanation—I mean the calling out of all able-bodied men under sixty years of age. For I fail to understand an order not to leave France, as applied to men who are not to be called on to defend the country. So I beg you will send me the best-authenticated information you can come by. I will not let you carry a rifle without shouldering mine alongside of you; and though I am a poor shot, you need not fear my being so clumsy as to shoot you by accident. We *must* be side by side, if there is any question of either of us going under fire. I have already told you so, and my own inaptitude for military duty has nothing to do or to say in the question. I have looked on the steps I have taken, up to this, as an absolute duty. That duty would become merely relative, consequently less, and therefore null and void, if another and a greater should appear to over-ride it.

Our poor beloved country is in a very serious position—worse, as far as I can see, than in any previous trial. Never before have the two great problems of external struggle and internal union loomed so urgent or so huge. I feel certain that internal union, in the face of the common enemy, does actually exist. Whether it is merely temporary, or whether it will continue after the struggle is over—whatever may be its issue—that's the question! Victor or vanquished, will France emerge a republic? In any case—whatever the resistance Paris makes, and her ultimate fate—it will be long, I think, before France is utterly devoured. The mouthful is a large one, and it may not turn out altogether easy to break up.

Well, we all send our affectionate love. All friendly messages to your kind hosts, and my affectionate respects to M. le Curé, whom I shall never forget.

IV

October 19, 1870, 12.30 P.M.

My Dear Ones,—We are just going out with Mrs. Brown, who is coming in her carriage to take us to the Crystal Palace. The fountains play to-day for the last time this season, and she has set her heart on our seeing them. As you may fancy, dear Pigny, I shall hardly realise what is going on before my eyes. I can see nothing but our country. I see it clearer, more incessantly than when I was within its borders!

Ah! dear friend, will no one rise up and lead our brave-hearted Frenchmen on some steady line of conduct? Failing that, even the most heroic courage will avail us nothing. See how, one by one, one after the other, as though by some strange unheard-of fate, they all fall into the jaws of that huge automaton, that monstrous hydra-headed artillery! Every one of them founders in that hostile ocean, dashing gallantly and ceaselessly against that ever-growing mountain of cannon, and shot, and shell, and strange engines of war, and battalions that seem to start ready armed out of the earth wherever the enemy chances to need them! and meanwhile our generals are being dismissed, or moved from one command to another,—they are left without orders, and thrown on their own resources, to take the chance of whatever their private or personal inspiration may dictate. Three thousand men cut up, to the last man, in a desperate hopeless defence of the Orléans railway station, all unconscious that the opposing force numbers five-and-thirty thousand!! Surely it is sheer madness thus to cast the blood, and bravery, and downright heroism of these splendid fellows into the outer darkness of what fate (or is it mere chance?) may bring!

We ought *all* to be standing face to face with the Prussians at this moment. Every one of us, or not a soul! And it astounds me that three million Frenchmen and thirty thousand cannon were not summoned, over a month ago, under one and the same flag (not that of France alone, but of humanity in general), to repulse this invasion of machines rather than of men! Here comes Mrs. Brown. Good-bye for awhile!

V

8 Morden Road, Blackheath Park,
Tuesday, November 8, 1870.

Dear Edouard,—We are just going to change houses again. We leave Morden Road next Saturday for London, where my work and engagements render my presence indispensable. I must get back to work—and to useful work. I cannot let myself pine and dwindle any longer in endless, hopeless sorrow. In another month I should be utterly incapable.

If I can write, and sell what I write, I will sell my work.

If I have to give lessons, I will teach: for the armistice is breaking down, and nobody knows what winter may bring with it. So our poor little flock is scattered, dear fellow! Not in heart indeed, but in body; and "Je ne suis pas de ceux qui disent ce n'est rien!... Je dis que c'est beaucoup!" as old La Fontaine has it.

Tell my dear little Guillaume how much his letters are treasured, not only by the loving heart of his grandmother, but by his uncle, who watches and follows every symptom of his tastes, every instinct of his nature, everything that bears upon his future, every thought—all those inner workings, in a word, which constitute the continuation of a youth's mental evolution and ultimate development—with an affectionate solicitude which I venture to call almost maternal. Everything I notice in him is good, and augurs well; and I believe the serious and even tragic events amid the tumult of which his young life has opened will have endued all his good qualities with a maturity which peace might only have brought them twenty years later.

Everybody here is well. Jean and Jeanne send their affectionate love to their uncle and cousin.

VI

My dear Pi,—So our hopes are dashed again, by the final rupture of the armistice, which, as it had seemed to me, was strengthened by all M. Thiers' consummate powers as a negotiator, and for which the Government was willing to make every concession to which a self-respecting nation could condescend.

And what will happen now? Alas! the thought overwhelms me. But though I cannot turn my heart and mind from the misfortunes of our beloved country, I feel I must make a desperate appeal to my powers of work, to my duty, to my *usefulness*. Useful I can be to my near and dear ones (for I must support them), and useful, too, to myself—for I must shake free of the slow agony which has been on me ever since we got here, and which would utterly consume me if I did not call together all my remaining strength, to make a struggle against the *invasion of my own morale*.

I shall therefore, as events seem likely, for some time to come, to render our return to France impossible, spend the winter in finishing, or at all events in carrying on my present work,[19] so that when the waters go back I may open the window of my ark and let my dove (which may perhaps turn out to be a raven!) fly out. In any case, it will mean that the rainbow has come back, and with it peace among the nations.

Would you were with us, my dear ones! How we are scattered this winter!

VII

LONDON, *December 24, 1870.*

DEAR FRIENDS,—This is the eve of a great day here, which English people keep as we do New Year's Day. And I must confess that to me Christmas, which brings back the greatest of all dates to our memory, opens the year much more appropriately than our "Jour de l'An." Alas! whichever way we take it, what a year of pain this which is just about to close has been, to each and all of us, parted as we are, after so many misfortunes endured, in anxieties such as still beset us, and amid the dread of what may yet befall us. Our very hearts have groaned and suffered for the last five months, unceasingly. For five whole months humanity has gazed on a horrid sight—the most merciless work of destruction, carried on in a century which proudly arrogates to itself the title of "Progress," but the memory of which will go down to posterity stained with the most revolting atrocities. What is progress, forsooth, but the onward march of intelligence, in the light of love? And what has this century done, I will not say for the pleasure, but for the happiness of the human race?

Napoleon I.! Napoleon III.! William of Prussia! Waterloo! mitrailleuses! Krupp guns!...

In what a scene of ruin shall we meet! We have been physically parted, but our hearts have never been severed! far from it! It seems as though this hard and cruel apprenticeship must knit us closer to everything that makes life real, and sure, and steadfast. So my heart yearns to yours now, in absence, more tenderly, more clingingly, than it ever did in happier times! We shall all feel our meeting even more than we should have if we had never been so far apart. Fondest love to each and all of you—to Berthe, to you, dear Pi, to all our friends.

VIII

December 28, 1870.

MY DEAR EDOUARD,—A sad New Year's Day we shall all have, scattered as we

[19] "Polyeucte." Gounod also wrote his "Gallia" at this period.

are, and have been for so long! Homeless, parted from our nearest and dearest, our friends all gone or scattered too, in constant anxiety about the wellbeing, the health, the very existence of those we love, thousands of lives cut off, and careers destroyed, or checked, or hampered—of families brought to ruin, provinces ravaged and harried, and nothing decisive to show at the end of it all. There you have the sum total, the last will and testament of this dying year, which has devoured countless victims, and spread disaster far and wide—the result at this present moment of "Human Progress." If the tree should be judged by its fruits, and if, as undoubtedly is the case, the value of a cause is to be measured by that of its effect, we must admit, considering what it has brought us to, that human wisdom has gone sadly astray, and that human reason, for the emancipation of which we have been so jealous, does no great credit either to its independence or its own teachings. If all our misfortunes end by giving us a lesson, by bringing us back to the simplicity of truth, and the truth of simplicity, they will not be utterly wasted, and we shall have gained a somewhat both precious and beneficent. For all things proceed from each other, here below; truth and falsehood each have their inevitable consequences. According to the tree, so shall its fruit be. What will the year 1871 bring us? I know not; but it seems to me it must be a decisive year, for good or for evil, not for us only, but for Europe—for what is known as the civilised world. We *must* learn at last *where* we really are. It is high time that the nations should make sure wherein their life lies, and their death—what their strength is, and their weakness—whence they may look for light, or darkness—how they may escape all temporary shifts, and settle down on firm and durable foundations. This is the method in all sciences; and politics is a science, which must have a basis and constructive system of its own.

Well, well! Best love to Anna and to grandmamma.

IX

Thursday, March 16, 1871.

Dearest Berthe,—Your letter of the 13th only reached us this morning. It has grieved us sorely. Our dreary winter will close sadly indeed, what with our dear mother's departure, the reasons which make that step wise and even necessary, the thought of how all she will see must wring her heart, and our own disappointment at not having you here for a while, as we had hoped.

If I was not bound until the 1st of May by the engagements I have made in London for that date, I should have started, and so would Anna and her children, with my mother. Duty, in the shape of earning a few crusts, forbids my moving yet, but we shall be on our way to join you before the first week in May is over. In spite of the very favourable welcome, and the artistic position my work has earned me here, I feel this country is not my France, and I believe, being a particularly human person, that my French nature and habits are too old to be modified by transplanting; I shall live and die essentially *a Frenchman*. The day is yet far distant when the sense of the whole earth being his fatherland will predominate in the heart of man over love for the soil of his country.

My tenderest greeting to you both.

X

LONDON, April 14, 1871.

DEAR FRIEND,—Your letter of the 12th has just reached me, and I reply at once, in the hope that my answer may be at Versailles in time to welcome you on your return to the dear fraternal roof, and that thus your two brothers may each greet you after his fashion—one in his peaceful garden, the other by these few lines from the other side of the sea; one opening his door to you, the other stretching out his arms; both taking you to their hearts. How large the place you hold there, you know right well! Alas! dear friend, dear brother, I too hear the terrible guns whose booming grieves your soul and breaks your heart, as well it may! As step by step I follow the progress of events, and the various phases of this conflict, or rather of the utter bedlam which causes and maintains it, I watch the gradual disappearance—I will not say of my illusions (the word is not worthy to express my meaning, nor should I mourn over it as I do), but of my hopes, present or near, at all events, of the approaching erection of a new *story* in the building of the moral habitation men call "Liberty," the only dwelling, after all, worthy of the human race. No, again I say it, these are no illusions which are fading from our sight! Liberty is no dream; it is our Canaan, a true land of promise. But, like the Jews, we shall only see it afar off. To enter it, we must become God's own people. Liberty is as real as heaven. It is a heaven on earth—the country of the elect; but it must be earned, and conquered, not by oppression, but by self-devotion; not by pillage, but by generosity; not by taking life, but by bestowing it, in the moral as well as the material sense. Morally, above all; for once that is well understood and ascertained, the material side of the question will take care of itself. The *man's* hygiene must come first, his animal welfare second—that is the just, and therefore the logical course.

When I consider the outcome (so far at least) of all the moral gifts, all the advances on trust, as it were, of which humanity, political and social, has been the recipient, up till this present day, I cannot help observing that it has been treated like a spoilt child. I feel inclined to doubt whether a wise and opportune distribution of all those gifts which cannot be appreciated and utilised till the human race comes of age, has not been anticipated with reckless and imprudent prodigality. We still stand in need of *overseers*. Well, master for master, take it all in all, I would rather have *one* than *two hundred thousand*. You can always get rid of one tyrant (natural death, what we call *la belle mort*, will do that for you); but a collective tyranny, compact, endlessly reproductive, feeding and fattening perpetually on its own victims!—I can never believe that is God's chosen model of human evolution. Now, if we carry the argument to its conclusion, we come to this: "Liberty is merely the voluntary and conscious accomplishment of justice." And as justice is obedience to eternal and unchanging laws, it follows that where there is freedom there must be submission. This is the end of the argument, and the basis of all life. I should go on twaddling for ever (and so would you), but I must not forget mine is not the only letter this envelope is to hold.

So I will send my affectionate love to you and Berthe.—Your brother,

CH. GOUNOD.

BERLIOZ

IN the ranks of human nature certain peculiarly sensitive beings are to be found, whom circumstances affect after a fashion utterly distinct, both in nature and degree, from the results they produce on other men. These individuals form the inevitable exception to an otherwise invariable rule. Their natural idiosyncrasies explain the peculiar features of their various lives, and to these lives again their ultimate fate may fairly be ascribed.

Now the exceptional men and women lead the world. This is inevitable, for their struggle and their suffering is the price of the enlightenment and progress of humanity at large. Once these intellectual pioneers have dropped on the road they have hewed out—oh! then troops up the flock of imitators, full of the pride of breaking down the already opened door; every separate sheep of them, as vainglorious as the legendary fly on the coach-wheel, loudly claiming the honour and glory of having won triumph for the Revolution. "J'ai tant fait que nos gens sont enfin dans la plaine!" Like Beethoven, Berlioz was one of the illustrious sufferers from that painful privilege of being an exceptional man. Dearly did he pay for the heavy responsibility! The exceptional man must suffer. Fate wills it thus, and, as invariably, he must bring suffering on others. How can the common herd (that *profanum vulgus* so execrated by the poet Horace) be expected to acknowledge its own incompetence and bow down before any insignificant though audacious person who dares stand out boldly against inveterate custom and the sovereign rule of old-established routine? Did not Voltaire (a clever man, if ever there was one) declare that no one person was as clever as all the rest put together? And is not universal suffrage, the great achievement of these modern days, the irrevocable verdict of the sovereign populace? Does not the voice of the people equal the voice divine?

History, meanwhile, with its steady onward march, which from time to time exposes many a counterfeit—history, I say, teaches us that everywhere, and invariably, light proceeds from the individual to the multitude, and never from the multitude to the individual; from the wise to the ignorant, never from the ignorant to the wise; from the sun to the planet, never from the planet to the sun. You cannot expect thirty-six millions of blind men to do the work of one telescope, or thirty-six millions of sheep that of one shepherd! Was it the world at large that formed Raphael and Michael Angelo, Mozart and Beethoven, Newton and Galileo? The world!—which spends its life making and unmaking its own judgments, in a perpetual alternate condemnation of its own infatuations and prejudices. How can the world judge anything? Would you erect such wavering contradictory decrees into an infallible jurisdiction? The very thought is laughable. The world's first impulse is to scourge and crucify. Long afterwards, in the next generation oftener than not, or a still later one, a tardy repentance reverses the judgment, and the laurels denied to the living genius fall like rain upon his tomb. The only true and definite sentence, that of posterity, is but the accumulated judgment of successive minorities. Majorities are the "preservers of the *statu quo*." I do not blame them. They probably fulfil their true function in the general order of things. They may keep the chariot back. They certainly do not help it onwards. They act as a drag, when they do not play the part of ruts upon the path. Immediate success is often enough a mere question of fashion. It proves a work to be on a level with the age; it by no means argues any long survival. There is no great reason, then, for being proud of it.

Berlioz was a very single-minded man, ignorant of all arts of concession or compromise. Belonging, as he did, to the race of *Alcestis*, naturally enough the hand of every *Orontes* was against him. And how many "Orontes" there are in this world! People called him crotchety, surly, quarrelsome, what not! But surely those who complained of this extreme sensitiveness, often amounting to excessive irritability, should have made some allowance for the annoyances, the personal suffering, the innumerable rebuffs endured by a proud-hearted man, to whom any mean compliance or cringing servility was utterly impossible. Though his opinions may have seemed hard and severe to those concerning whom they were expressed, they never, at all events, can be attributed to any shameful or jealous motive. Such feelings were quite incompatible with the nobility of that great and generous and loyal nature. The trials endured by Berlioz when competing for the Grand Prix de Rome were the faithful image, and, as it were, the prophetic prelude to those he was to face all through his career. He actually competed four times over, and he was twenty-seven when, by dint of his own perseverance, and in spite of the innumerable difficulties he had to overcome, he won the prize, in the year 1830.

The very year which saw him carry off the prize with his cantata "Sardanapale" also saw the execution of a work which demonstrated the point his artistic development (so far as musical conception, colour, and experience are concerned) had reached. His "Symphonic Fantastique" ("episode dans la vie d'un artiste") was a real event in the musical world, the importance of which may be gauged by the fanatical admiration and the violent opposition it aroused. Admitting that a work of such a nature may be open to much discussion, the fact that its composer possessed most remarkable inventive power, and a powerful poetic sentiment (which reappears in all his subsequent compositions), still remains evident.

Berlioz has put into musical circulation, so to speak, a large number of orchestral effects and combinations which were unknown before his time, and which have been adopted by very illustrious musicians indeed. He has revolutionised the art of instrumentation, and in that respect, at all events, may be said to have "founded a school." And yet, in spite of certain brilliant successes both in France and elsewhere, his whole life was a struggle. In spite of performances to which his personal guidance as an orchestral conductor of great eminence and his indefatigable energy added many chances of success and many elements of brilliance, his personal public was always a limited one. The great public, that "everybody" which turns *success* into *popularity*, never knew him. Popularity was so slow in coming to Berlioz that he died of the delay. The end came at last, with the "Troyens," a work which, as he foresaw, caused him a world of sorrow. Like his namesake and his hero, he may be said to have perished before the walls of Troy. Every impression, every sensation Berlioz underwent was carried to an extreme. He knew no joy or sorrow short of downright delirium. As he himself would say, he was a "volcano." Extreme sensibility carries one as far in suffering as in delight. Tabor and Golgotha are not far apart. Happiness no more consists in the absence of suffering than genius implies freedom from all faults.

Men of genius must and do suffer, but they need no pity. They know raptures which are a sealed book to others, and if they have wept for sadness, they have shed tears of ineffable joy as well. That in itself constitutes a heaven that can never be too dearly bought.

Berlioz was one of the greatest emotional influences of my youth. Older than myself by fifteen years, he was a man of four-and-thirty when I, a lad of nineteen, studied composition under Halévy at the Conservatoire. I recollect the impression his person and his works (which he often rehearsed in the concert-room of the Conservatoire) produced on me. The moment Halévy had corrected my work I used to fly from the class-room, and lie low in some corner of the concert-hall, and there remain, intoxicated by the weird, passionate, tumultuous strains, which seemed to open new and brilliant worlds to me. One day, I remember, I had been listening to a rehearsal of his "Romeo and Juliet" Symphony, then unpublished, and which was shortly to be given in public for the first time. I was so struck by the grandeur and breadth of the great finale of the "Reconciliation des Montaigus et des Capulets," that when I left the hall my memory retained the whole of Friar Lawrence's splendid phrase, "Jurez tous par l'auguste symbole." A few days afterwards I went to see Berlioz, and sitting down to the piano, I played the whole passage over to him. He opened his eyes very wide, and looking hard at me, he asked—

"Where the devil did you hear that?"

"At one of your rehearsals," I replied. He could hardly believe his ears.

The sum total of Berlioz' work is very considerable. Thanks to the initiative of two courageous orchestral leaders (M. Jules Pasdeloup and M. Édouard Colonne), the present public has already become acquainted with several of the great composer's vast conceptions—the "Symphonic Fantastique," the "Romeo and Juliet" Symphony, the "Harold Symphony," the "Enfance du Christ," three or four great overtures, and, above all, that magnificent work the "Damnation de Faust," which in the course of the last two years has roused such transports of enthusiasm as would have stirred the artist's very ashes, if the dead could stir. But what a mine remains yet unexplored! Shall we never hear his "Te Deum," in all its grandeur of conception? And will no director produce that charming opera, "Beatrix et Bénédict?" Such an attempt nowadays, when opinion has so veered round to Berlioz' side, would have every chance of success. Though no particular merit on the score of risk encountered could be claimed, it might be wise to seize the favourable opportunity. The following letters have a double charm. They are all unpublished hitherto, and every one of them has been written in the spirit of absolute sincerity, which is the eternally indispensable condition of true friendship. Some may deplore the lack of deference they betray with respect to men whose talents should apparently shield them from irreverent and unjust description. People will say, and not unreasonably, that Berlioz would have done better not to style Bellini a "little blackguard," and that the appellation of "illustrious old gentleman" as applied to Cherubini, with evidently ill-natured intent, was very inappropriate to the eminent composer whom Beethoven considered the greatest of his age, and to whom he, Beethoven, the mighty symphonist, paid the signal honour of humbly submitting the MS. of the "Messe Solennelle" (Op. 123), with the request that he would freely express his opinion concerning it. Be that as it may, and in spite of blots for which the writer's cross-grained temper is alone responsible, the letters are most deeply interesting. Berlioz bares his heart in them, as it were. He lets himself go; he enters into the most intimate details of his private and artistic life. In a word, he opens his whole heart to his friend, and that in terms of such effusive warmth and affection as prove how worthy each was of the other's friendship, and how complete the mutual understanding was. To understand each other! How the word calls up that immortal fable of our heaven-sent La Fontaine, "Les deux Amis."

To understand! to enter into that perfect communion of heart and thought and interest to which we give the two fairest names in human language—friendship and love. Therein lies life's whole charm, and the most powerful attraction, too, in that *written life,* that conversation betwixt parted friends which is so appropriately known as "correspondence."

The musical works of Berlioz may earn him glory. The published letters will do more. They will earn him love, and that is the most precious of all earthly things.

Charles Gounod.

M. CAMILLE SAINT-SAËNS AND HIS OPERA "HENRI VIII."

WHEN, after years of perseverance and struggle, a highly gifted artist gains the exalted place in public opinion to which he is justly entitled, everybody, even his most obstinate opponent, exclaims, "Didn't I always say people would end by coming round?"

Five and twenty years ago, or more (for he came out as an infant prodigy), M. Saint-Saëns made his first appearance in the musical world. How many times since then have I been told: "Saint-Saëns? Eh? Now really? Oh, as a pianist or an organist, I dare say. But as a composer! Do you really and truly think?..." And all the rest of the usual stereotyped phrases. Well, I *did* think so, really and truly; and I was not the only person who did. Now everybody else thinks so too. Misgivings have all faded away, prejudices are all dispelled—M. Saint-Saëns has won. He has only to say, "J'y suis, j'y reste," and he will be one of the glories of his time and of his art.

According to admitted opinion among certain artists, if a man speaks well of a brother artist's work, the natural inference is that he thinks ill of it, and *vice versâ*. But why? Must you refuse to admit other men's talent or genius in order to prove your own? Did Beethoven slay Mozart? Will Rossini prevent Mendelssohn from living on? Do you believe that, as Celimène says in the play, "C'est être savant que trouver à redire"?

Are you afraid there will not be room enough for you? Pray calm that fear! There will always be room and to spare in the Temple of Fame. If your place is marked there, it awaits you. The great point is that you should come and take it.

No; the real dread is that of not being foremost Alack! this fretful, nervous preoccupation concerning relative value is the very antithesis of real merit. It is the same shabby old story—love of self usurping the place and duty of love in the true sense. Let us love our art. Let us fight, in all honesty and boldness, for any man or woman who serves it bravely and nobly. Let us not hold truth "captive in the hand of injustice." That which we strive to conceal to-day will surely be in public knowledge on the morrow. The only honourable course is to prepare that judgment of posterity, the *vox populi, vox Dei,* which ranks no man by favour, or, what is worse, by interest, but gives sentence in true justice, infallible and eternal.

To keep back the truth, proves that we do not love it. To grieve because some other man serves truth better than ourselves, proves that we would have the honour due to truth alone paid to our own persons.

Let us rather do all we can to diffuse the light of truth. We never can have too much of it.

M. Saint-Saëns is one of the most astonishingly gifted men, as regards musical powers, I have ever met with. He is armed at all points. He knows his business thoroughly. I need only remark that he uses his orchestra, and plays with it, just as he plays on and with his piano.

He possesses the gift of description in the highest and rarest degree. He has an enormous power of assimilation. He can write you a work in any style you choose—Rossini's, Verdi's, Schumann's, Wagner's. He knows them all thoroughly—the surest safeguard, it may be, against his imitating any. He never suffers from that bugbear of the chicken-hearted, the dread of not making his effect. He never exaggerates; thus he is never far-fetched, nor violent, nor over-emphatic. He uses every combination and every resource without abuse, and without being enslaved by any one of them.

He is no pedant. There is no solemnity, no *transcendentalism* about him. He is too childish still, and has grown far too wise, for that. He has no special system; he belongs to no party or clique. He does not set up to be a reformer of any sort. He writes as he *feels* and *knows*. Mozart was no reformer either, and, as far as I am aware, that fact has not prevented his reaching the highest pinnacle of his art.

Another virtue (and one I desire to emphasise in these days), M. Saint-Saëns writes music *that keeps time*, without perpetually dragging out over those silly and detestable pauses which make any proper musical construction impossible, and which are a mere maudlin affectation. He is simply a thoroughbred musician, who draws and paints with all the freedom of a master-hand; and if originality consists in never imitating another, there can be no doubt about it in his case.

I do not propose in this place to go into all the details of the libretto of "Henri VIII." The various newspaper reports of the first performance have already performed that duty; and besides, the story (I had almost said of that crowned hog!) of that practised Bluebeard and conceited and contemptible theologian is known to everybody. Nothing less than the triple crown sufficed his ambition, and the thought of the Pope disturbed his mind as much, at all events, as any woman, or strong drink, even.

But storm and threats availed him nothing. The Papacy has been blustered at in every key, but it still slumbers on peacefully in its bark, which no tempest seems able to submerge.

M. Saint-Saëns has given us no overture to this opera. This is certainly not because he lacked symphonic skill. Of that he has already given us superabundant proof. The work opens with a prelude based on an English theme, which will reappear as the principal one in the finale of the third act.

This prelude introduces us to the actual drama. In the very first scene, between Norfolk and Don Gomez, the Spanish Ambassador to Henry VIII.'s Court, a charming air occurs, "La beauté que je sers." It has a ring of youth about it, and the close, on the words, "Bien que je ne la nomme pas," is quite exquisitely simple.

In the first act the most remarkable numbers are a chorus of gentlemen discussing Buckingham's sentence; the King's air, "Qui donc commande quand il aime?" wonderfully truthful in expression; Anne Boleyn's *entrée*—a graceful *ritournelle,* leading up to a charming chorus for female voices, "Salut à toi qui nous viens de la France," which is followed by a passage quite out of the common both as regards the music itself and the scenic effect. I refer to the funeral march, when Buckingham is borne to his last home, in which the *De Profundis* is interwoven in a superlatively talented manner with the asides of the King and of Anne Boleyn in front; while the orchestra, as well as the monarch, whispers the caressing phrase which is to reappear in the course of the opera, "Si tu savais comme je t'aime!" in the young maid-of-honour's ear. This fine scene closes with a masterly ensemble, treated with great dramatic breadth, and which fitly and nobly crowns the first act.

The second act is laid in Richmond Park. It opens with a charming prelude—exquisitely dainty and clear in instrumentation—introducing a delightful theme which reappears later on in the duet between the King and Anne Boleyn, one of the most remarkable passages in the whole score.

After a soliloquy for Don Gomez, offering some fine opportunities for declamation, Anne Boleyn appears, with the ladies of the Court, who offer her flowers. This scene is full of charm and refinement. Then comes a short scene for Anne and Don Gomez, and then her great duet with the King. This duet is a very remarkable piece of writing. It throbs with impatient sensuality, concealed by an instrumentation full of the suggestion of feline caresses. The last ensemble is exquisite—well-nigh unapproachable in sonority and charm. The next air, "Reine! je serai reine!" gives a fine impression of a woman's intoxicated pride. In the duet between Anne Boleyn and Katherine of Aragon the expression given to the feelings of that noble-minded, unhappy Queen, alternately proud and tenderly forgiving, is very striking.

The third act represents the Council Chamber. It opens with a stately march, accompanying the entrance of the Court and the Judges. Then commences a superb full chorus, "Toi qui veilles sur l'Angleterre," after which Henry VIII. addresses the Synod, "Vous tous qui m'écoutez, gens d'Eglise et de loi!" Katherine, sorely agitated, scarcely able to speak, advances, and beseeches the King to have pity on her. This passage, in which the chorus occasionally joins, is most true and touching in feeling. In the face of the King's cruel scorn of his unhappy Queen, Don Gomez rises, and declares that as a Spaniard he undertakes the defence of his mistress. In his rage, Henry VIII. appeals to his subjects, "les fils de la noble Angleterre," who proclaim themselves ready to accept the decree of Heaven, about to be delivered by the Archbishop of Canterbury: "Nous déclarons nul et contraire aux lois, l'hymen à nous soumis."

Katherine rebels, and in a transport of indignant pride she cries, "Peuple que de ton roi déshonore le crime—tu ne te lèves pas!"

This passage is very striking and impressive. Katherine appeals to posterity, and goes out with Don Gomez.

The Legate enters, and then comes the great scene with which the third act closes.

In his hand the Legate holds the Papal Bull—

"Au nom de Clément VII. pontife souverain."

The King, driven to extremities, commands that the Palace gates shall be thrown open, and the populace admitted.

"Vous plait-il recevoir des lois de l'étranger?
Non! Jamais!
Vous convient-il qu'un homme
Dont le vrai pouvoir est à Rome
Sur mon trône ose m'outrager?
Non! Jamais!

And the King proclaims himself Head of the English Church, and takes Anne Boleyn, Marchioness of Pembroke, to wife!

This splendidly managed scene winds up with a stirring chorus, "C'en est donc fait! il a brisé sa chaine," worked out on the theme of the national air already appearing in the prelude which takes the place of overture to the opera.

The fourth act is also divided into two parts. The first is laid in Anne Boleyn's chamber. The curtain rises on a graceful song and dance, during which Norfolk and Surrey carry on an aside conversation very ingeniously interwoven with the dance-music. The next scene, between Anne and Don Gomez, has a charming air, sung with much expression by M. Dereims. A dialogue between the King and Don Gomez closes this first part.

The second shows us a huge apartment in the banished Queen Katherine's lodging at Kimbolton Castle. The touch of a master-hand is evident all through these closing scenes of M. Saint-Saëns' opera. They are instinct with incomparable power.

There is an admirable truth and sincerity in the Queen's soliloquy, full of tender and mournful expression. She presently distributes some of her belongings as keepsakes to her waiting-women. This little scene, almost domestic in its familiarity, is ennobled by the deep feeling with which the author has inspired it. Thus does truth elevate everything it touches!

Next comes the magnificent scene between Queen Katherine and Anne Boleyn. Mdlle. Krauss's comprehension and rendering of the Queen's superb note of indignation marked the consummate tragedian; her acting of the part rose to a striking level both of expression and of power.

The final numbers of this second and closing part form what is known in theatrical parlance as the *clou* of the drama. It is overwhelming. Never did curtain fall on anything more thrilling. Situation, music, singing, acting, all contribute to the powerful impression caused by this splendid scene—which called forth thunders of applause.

Such, as far as so hasty a description can give any idea of it, is M. Camille Saint-Saëns' new work.

As for the performers—every one of them fully equal to their task—we must first mention those who played the three principal parts: Mdlle. Krauss (Katharine of Aragon), Mdlle. Richard (Anne Boleyn), and M. Lassalle (Henry VIII.). Next come M. Boudouresque (the Papal Legate), M. Dereims (Don Gomez), M. Lorrain (Norfolk), M. Sapin (Surrey), and M. Gaspard (Archbishop of Canterbury).

Mdlle. Krauss was full of grandeur, nobility, and royal dignity. Both as actress and as singer, she proved her wonderful power of pathos. In the final scene especially, she sang, acted, *suffered,* with a truthfulness and intensity of expression which literally overwhelmed the onlookers with the sense of its reality. What a splendid artiste! What numberless parts she has identified with herself! How gallantly she plays them all! What a place she holds on our stage! What a void her absence would leave!

The part of Anne Boleyn gave Mdlle. Richard the opportunity of displaying all the charm of her full and beautiful voice, the rich tone of which is never strained by the wisely and well written music of her part.

M. Lassalle gave that of Henry VIII. all the interest of his clear diction and articulation; of a play that was sometimes gloomy and forbidding and sometimes impassioned; and of that rare voice of his, equally gifted in every shade of strength and softness.

M. Boudouresque would seem to have been born to be a Cardinal (*pace* the diabolic Bertram and the Huguenot Marcel, whom he represents so skilfully)! He looks as if he had been sent into the world to play Princes of the Church—*vide* Brogni in "La Juive," and this Papal Legate in "Henri VIII.," whom he invests with most imposing dignity.

M. Dereims, as Don Gomez, was remarkable for elegance and charm.

The orchestra, under M. Altès, was admirable; as was also the chorus, carefully taught and led by M. Jules Cohen.

M. Vaucorbeil, too, deserves a place of honour. He believed in M. Saint-Saëns, and as soon as he became Director of the Opera, he expressed a desire to see his work on our chief lyric stage. As is his custom, the truly artistic Director devoted all his intelligent care and attention to producing this noble and serious work; while yet another true artist, M. Régnier, gave it the benefit of all the scenic experience his long and brilliant theatrical career has brought him.

So, dear Saint-Saëns, you now behold your name linked with a work which has earned most signal honour for French art and for our National Academy of Music. To those who knew you as a child (myself among the number) your destiny was never doubtful. Musically speaking, you never had any childhood. Watchfully cherished as you were by your wise and noble-hearted mother, your earliest years were nourished by the great masters of your art. They set your feet boldly and firmly on your onward path. Your reputation has long since outstripped that order of popularity which is apparently the special privilege of the dramatic stage. The only thing lacking to give it weight was a brilliant theatrical success. That is now yours.

Forward then, dear and great musician! You have won all along the line. Posterity will be faithful to your work, because you are true to your art! God has gifted you with the master's knowledge and the master-hand! May they long be preserved to you, for your sake and for ours!

NATURE AND ART

Paper read by M. CHARLES GOUNOD, *Member of the Académie des Beaux Arts, at the Annual Public Meeting of the Five Académies, October* 23, 1886.

Gentlemen,—The successive transformations of which this earth has been the scene, and which form its history—I had almost said its education—since it dropped from its place amongst the solar nebulæ to take up a more distinct position in space, are so many chapters, as it were, in that great law of progress, that perpetual *tending*, which seems to draw all creation towards some mysterious goal, and whose various phases have been summed up in three general orders which have been designated *ages*, and which denote the three hitherto most evident phases of existence on our globe. But the book was not closed here, and earth's history was not to end with these three earliest forms of life. A fourth, the Human Age (for thus science permits me to call it), was to reign in this unconscious kingdom. The huge travail of evolution, the tremendous effort of parturition in which the plan of the Creator is unfolded, was to be taken up by man at the point to which his forerunners had carried it, and to be brought, by the exercise of nobler functions, to a yet higher destiny. The law of life, of which earth's creatures had so far been the more or less passive but utterly irresponsible depositaries, was to be *confided* to man's care, he being raised to the supreme honour of voluntarily accomplishing its known behest—an honour constituting the essential idea of liberty, and which instantly transforms instinctive activity into rational or conscious action. In a word, Morality (or the definition of what is good), Science (or the definition of what is true), Art (or the definition of what is beautiful), were all lacking until the advent of Man. And Man, in his quality of high priest of a temple, thenceforward dedicated to Goodness, Beauty, and Truth, was destined to dower and glorify the world by their bestowal.

What, then, is an artist? What is his function with regard to this conception of Nature, and, as I may almost say, this investment of her capital?

Man's sublime function is literally and positively that of a *new earthly Creator*. His duty is to *make* all things what they ought to *become*. Not merely in the matter of the cultivation of the soil of our earth, but also as regards intellectual and moral culture—justice, love, science, arts, trade and manufactures—no consummation nor true conclusion is possible save through Man, to whom creation was confided that he might *till it*—"ut operatur terram," as the old text of the Book of Genesis runs. An artist, then, is not simply a sort of mechanical apparatus which receives or reflects the image of exterior and visible objects; he is a sensitive and living instrument, which wakes to consciousness and vibrates at the touch of Nature. And this vibration it is which at once indicates the artistic vocation, and is the primary cause of any work of art.

Necessarily called into existence, in the first place, by the fostering rays of a personal sentiment, a true work of art must reach its perfect form in the full and impersonal light of reason. Art is concrete and visible reality, glorified by that other abstract and intelligible reality which the artist bears within himself, and which is his ideal; that is to say, the inner revelation, the supreme tribunal, the ever-growing vision of ultimate possibility after which the whole fervour of his being strives.

If it were possible for the artist to lay hands on his ideal—to gaze on it face to face, in all its complete reality—its reproduction would be reduced to a mere matter of copying. This would amount to downright realism, superlative of its kind no doubt, but positive; and thus the two factors of the artist's work—the personal function, which constitutes its *originality*, and the æsthetic one, which constitutes its *rationality*—are at once eliminated. This is not the true relation between the work of art and the artist's ideal conception. The ideal can never be adequately reproduced. It is the loadstar, the motive force. The artist feels it, he is ruled by it, it is his undefined "excelsior," the imperious *desideratum* imposed on him by the law of Beauty, and the very persistence of its inner prompting proves its truth and the impossibility of its attainment.

To draw from an imperfect and lower reality the elements which shall measure and determine the extent to which the said reality agrees or disagrees with Nature's reasonable law, herein lies the artist's highest function. And this verification of Nature as it is, by Nature's own laws, is what is known as "Æsthetics." "Æsthetics" are the argument of *Beauty*.

In art, as elsewhere, reason must counter-balance passion, and thence it follows that all artistic work of the very highest class leaves an impress of calm—that sign of real power, which "rules its art even to the checking point."

As we have already observed, it is the *personal* emotion, in the artist's collaboration with Nature, which gives the stamp of *originality* to his work. Originality is often confounded with peculiarity or oddity. Yet they are absolutely distinct qualities. Oddity is something abnormal, even unhealthy. It is a mitigated form of mental alienation, and belongs to the region of pathology. As the synonymous word eccentricity so well denotes, it is a deviation, a running off at a tangent.

Originality, on the other hand, is the distinctly evident link which binds the individual to the common intellectual centre. The work of art is the progeny of the common mother—Nature; and of a distinct father—the artist. Its originality is simply an asseveration of paternity. It is the proper name linked to the family appellation, an individual recommendation approved by the community at large.

But the artist's work does not consist merely in his personal expression, though that indeed gives it its distinctive quality, its individual features, even while it thereby confines them within certain limits.

As a matter of fact, while his artistic sensitiveness brings him into touch with actual nature, his reason brings him into equal contact with ideal nature, and this in virtue of that law of transfiguration which must be applied to all existent realities, so as to draw them ever closer to those which *are*—in other words, to their perfect prototype.

Let me here quote a sentence which seems to me, at all events, a somewhat striking formulation, even if it be not a proof, of the truth of the foregoing remarks. St. Theresa, that pious woman whose brilliant wisdom has earned her a place amongst the most famous teachers of the Church, used to say she did not remember ever to have heard a bad sermon. I ask no better than to believe this, seeing she said it. But it must be admitted that unless the saint deceived herself, she herself at least, if not the period in which she lived, must have been blessed with some special favour, by no means the lightest, in all conscience, which God has been pleased to bestow upon His faithful servants. However that may have been, and without desiring to cast the slightest doubt on the faithfulness of her witness, it may be explained—translated, let us say; and we may arrive at some comprehension of how, and to what an occasionally astounding extent, the inaccurate relation of a fact may co-exist with the absolute veracity of the person who bears the testimony.

Why did St. Theresa never recollect having heard a bad sermon? Because every sermon she heard with her outward ears was spontaneously transfigured, and literally *recreated* by reason of the sublimity of that which sounded ever within her own soul. Because the words of the preacher, void though they might be of literary power or oratorical artifice, spoke to her of that which she loved best in the world, and once her spirit was borne in that direction, or to that level, she felt and heard nothing but God—concerning whom the preacher spoke.

"Use my eyes," said a famous painter, when an acquaintance complained of the hideousness of his model; "use my eyes, sir, and you will see he is sublime!"

Thus, at the mere sight of even a second-rate work, so that it suffice to kindle that divine spark, the hall-mark of genius, in his soul, the truly great artist will suddenly grasp his idea, and fathom the very depths of his art in one swift piercing glance.

Who can tell whether the "Barbier de Seville" and "Guillaume Tell" were not cradled on the paternal trestle stage on which Rossini's musical training first began?

To pass from exterior tangible realities to emotion, from emotion onwards to reason, this is the progressive order of true intellectual development. And this it is which St Augustine sums up so admirably in one of those clear and perspicuous maxims constantly to be met with in his works: "Ab exterioribus ad interiora, ab interioribus ad superiora"—From without, within; from within, above.

Art is one of the three incarnations of the ideal in the real; one of the three operations of that spirit which is to "renew the face of the earth;" one of the three revivals of Nature in man; one of the three forms, in a word, of that principle of separate immortality which constitutes the perpetual resurrection of humanity at large, by virtue of its three creative powers, distinct in function, though substantially identical—viz., Love, the essence of human life; Science, the essence of truth; and Art, the essence of beauty.

Having thus endeavoured to show how the law which governs the progress of the human mind resides in the union of the ideal with the real, it now remains for me to give the counter-proof, by demonstrating the result of the separation and isolation of these two factors.

In art, mere realism is another word for slavish imitation. Utter idealism is the madness of fancy. In science, reality, by itself, is the enigma of fact unenlightened by its laws. Idealism alone is a ghostly conjecture, devoid of the confirmation of actualities.

In morality, realism unadulterated means the egotism of self-interest—in other words, a lack of *rational* sanction in the field of human will. Unmixed idealism is mere Utopia, or the absence of the sanction of experience in all that is governed by human maxims.

In each and every case there must be either a soulless body or a disembodied soul; a denial of the law of existence by one who belongs at once, by virtue of his double nature, to the tangible and to the intellectual order of life, and whose being is only normal and complete inasmuch as it gives expression to these two orders of reality. If there be one peculiarity specially characteristic of these three high human vocations, the service of Goodness, of Beauty, and of Truth—if there be a bond between them, which marks the divinity of their common origin, and raises them to truly Apostolic dignity—it is that they are disinterested, gratuitous, *freely given*.

The functions of *life* are so closely knit to those of *existence* that the divine freedom of a man's vocation must perforce submit to the human necessities of his profession. And the most passionate and eager *livers* often understand little, and fare ill, when it comes to matters of *subsistence*. But all the superior functions of mankind are necessarily and intrinsically *gratuitous*.

Neither Love, nor Science, nor Art can be venally appraised. They are the divine three persons of the human conscience. Only finite things can be sold. Immortal things must bestow themselves freely.

Therefore it is that the handiwork of Goodness, of Beauty, and of Truth defies the centuries; the very eternity of their first causes gives them life.

"NEW HEAVENS AND A NEW EARTH."

Thus did the mighty captive of Patmos, the prince of evangelists, foretell the end of time, in the twenty-first chapter of the Apocalypse; a stately vision, culminating in the hosannah of the "New Jerusalem, the Holy City, coming down from God out of heaven prepared as a bride adorned for her husband." What mighty seers they were! those great Hebrew poets! those diviners of the growth and destinies of the human race!—Job, David, Solomon, the Prophets, St. Paul, and the Apostle John, who was permitted to learn the secrets of eternity and to peer into the unfathomable depths of infinite generations!

That New Jerusalem, that chosen country, is *human selection,* the victorious solver of all enigmas, bearing, like some glorious trophy, all the sacramental veils the world has dropped one by one along the centuries—"the faithful steward entering into the joy of his Lord," who, under the glorious light of the "New Heaven," lays the "New Earth" regenerated, *recreated,* according to the law expressed in the supreme formula: "Verily, I say unto you, Except a man be born again he can in no case enter into the kingdom of heaven"—at the feet of his Father and his God.

THE ACADEMY OF FRANCE AT ROME

AT a juncture like the present, when, under the mask of so-called *naturalism* in Art, an effort is being made to cast disfavour upon that noble and beneficent institution, the Academy of France in Rome, it appears to me a duty to enter a protest against the destructive tendencies, which, could they aspire to the dignity of being called doctrines, would end in nothing short of the utter obliteration of the Fine Arts, in their highest sense, and which, moreover, have no foundation save in the very emptiest and most frivolous of arguments. The advocates of what *they* denominate "Modern Art" (as if Art did not belong to all times) make an unconditional attack on the École de Rome; and their ultimatum is that the Villa Medicis, being a hotbed of artistic infection, must be forthwith done away with. This constitutes the "delenda Carthago" of the Anti-Roman party.

I shall not here undertake to plead *ex professo* in favour of the painters, sculptors, architects, and engravers whom the State sends year by year to Rome, thus ensuring them, in return for the hopes their talent has excited, constant and assiduous communion with the immortal teachers of the past, known as "the Masters." Myself a musician, I will confine myself to the points affecting the interests of musical composers, the more so as in their case especially a residence in Rome is looked on as being utterly useless and meaningless. But, seeing the cause of one art is the cause of Art in general, anything I may say about musicians will naturally apply to all other artists.

The first thing that strikes me is the fact that this bitterness against the Roman school is the mere outcome of a desire, more or less frankly expressed, which sums up in itself the whole of the opposition programme. "Down with the teachers! Let us use our own wings!" There is no doubt this is what is meant by "Modern Art."

No more education, then; no more acquired and transmissible ideas. That means no capital, and therefore no more patrimony nor inheritance. No past, therefore, no more traditions, no more intellectual paternity. In other words, the reign of spontaneous generation. For there is nothing between the two. We must have either teaching or intuitive knowledge. And note well that those who hug this system are the very men who are always talking about "the School of the Future." By what right, I ask, do they invoke the Future, when within a few days they must have become in its eyes that very Past they will have none of? A wonderfully absurd self-contradiction, this "kingdom divided against itself!" Show me any single method of employing human faculties which rests on such a theory! Law? Physical science? Chemistry? Astronomy? Mechanics? Is not man primarily an *educated* being? Does not his whole existence depend on an amassed capital of knowledge? Is he not taught to read, and write, and ride, and walk, and use weapons, and play on various instruments? Has not each department its own special form of gymnastics? And what is a school, after all, but a gymnasium?

Well, you say, let us grant all that, as far as science is concerned, and handicraft. But how about genius? No one can learn to be a genius. You either have that gift or have it not, and it can no more be bestowed on him who has it not than it can be taken from him who has it. That is a true and uncontested fact. But it is no less true that, as a great artist,[20] well qualified to speak, once said, "Art without science does not exist."

Genius, indeed, is incommunicable, for it is an essentially personal *gift*. But that which is communicable and transmissible is the language whereby genius is formulated and expressed, and failing which it must e'en remain dumb and impotent. Were not Raphael, Mozart, Beethoven, all men of genius? Did they conceive that fact authorised their scornful rejection of the traditional masters, who not only initiated them into the *practice* of their art, but also pointed them the surest *road* to follow, thus saving the immense waste of time involved in seeking a certainty already assured to them by the experience of past centuries? This claim to upset historical truths by dint of sheer sophistry is a downright mockery of common-sense. It amounts to asserting that no orator nor author need learn his language nor study his syntax and his dictionary. Théophile Gautier was right when he said, "If I write better than other people, it is because I have *learnt my business*, and I have a greater number of words at my command."

But, say the objectors, there are numbers of eminent artists who never studied at Rome at all.

This is perfectly true, and I hasten to add a fact, on which the opposition has no particular reason to plume itself so very proudly—that it by no means necessarily follows that a student at the École de Rome should emerge from it a very superior artist. But what does this prove? That Rome cannot perform a miracle and bestow what Nature has withheld. This is clear as daylight. It really would be too much to expect genius to be obtained at the price of a journey which anybody is free to make. But that is not the question at all. The question really is, whether, granted the possession of an artistic organisation, the influence Rome exercises thereon is not incontestable and unrivalled, in the matter of intellectual elevation and artistic development.

This view leads me to consider the utility of a residence in Rome as regards musical composers.

We will admit, the opposition say, that painters, sculptors, architects, and engravers should be sent to Italy. They will there find a considerable number of masterpieces, deeply interesting at all events, in connection with the different arts they practise. But what is a musician to do at Rome? What music is he to listen to? What *artistic* benefit can he gain there?

The fact is, that the people who make such objections must have given very little thought to the subject of what an artist is. Do they really believe he is given over

[20] Monsieur Ingres.

utterly to *technique*, as though mechanical proficiency constituted his whole art? As if a man might not be a clever mechanical performer and yet a commonplace artist; a consummate rhetorician, and a poor writer, or a cold speaker!

What! are eloquence and virtuosity one and the same thing? Is there no difference betwixt the man and the instrument he uses? Have men forgotten that the *artisan* is but part of the *artist*, that is, the *man*—that it is the *man* who must be touched, enlightened, carried away, nay, transfigured, so that he shall be lost in passionate adoration of that immortal beauty which ensures not momentary success alone, but the never-ending empire of those masterpieces which have been the light and guide of human art from the ancients down through the Renaissance to our own time, and will endure after it, and for ever!

Is this a real or merely a feigned ignorance of those immutable laws of nutrition and assimilation which govern the growth and perfect development of every organism? If music is the only thing necessary to the development and maturity of a musician's talent, I would not only ask why he should be sent to Rome, since there is no object in his gazing on the frescoes of Raphael and Michael Angelo on the Vatican hill, the home of all the oracles? I would fain know why he should read Homer, Virgil, Tacitus, Juvenal, Dante and Shakespeare, Molière and La Fontaine, Bossuet and Pascal—all, in a word, of the great nurturers of formulated human thought? What is the use? Literature is not music.... No! in good truth. But it is Art, which is ancient and modern too. Art, universal and eternal. And in Art the artist (not the artisan) must find his food, his health, his power, his very life. After all, what is this so-called *naturalism* in Art? I confess I should be glad to be informed as to the sense attached to the word by those who seem inclined to make it the banner of a grievance, and the symbol of a claim to a right denied by despotic routine. Does it mean that Nature should be the foundation and starting point in all art? In that sense all the Masters are agreed. But Art cannot stop there, and Raphael, whom I suppose I may take to have known Nature well, gives us the following definition, as admirable as it is perhaps over-spontaneous: "Art does not consist in representing things as Nature *made* them, but as she *should* have made them!" Sublime words, telling us clearly that Art is above all a preference, a true *selection*, and thus presupposing a training of the artist's understanding to a special standard of appreciation.

If Nature is everything, and education counts for nothing—if the common herd knows as much as the Masters, then how comes it that time so constantly reverses those ephemeral judgments which have so often showered transports of applause on works soon to be forgotten, or looked askance on masterpieces which have since been hailed with admiration by the infallible verdict of posterity?

I freely admit that the general public may be competent to judge a *play*—and even this may be contested when one remembers what an immense number of works held our fathers spell-bound, and leave us cold and indifferent. But even allowing for these ups and downs of popularity, it cannot be said that Art resides in the drama only. There is not the faintest analogy between the violent shock caused by some striking theatrical situation and the calm and noble delight to be derived from an exquisite and perfect work of art. Nobody could think of comparing the feelings produced by a melodrama to the emotion roused by a contemplation of the Frieze of the Parthenon, or the "Dispute du St Sacrement." A whole abyss lies betwixt the domain of mere sensation and that of intellectual feeling.

And what shall I say concerning the incalculable benefits to be found in the quietness and security of such a retreat, far from the feverish roar and constant anxiety of daily life? What of the silence, which teaches a man to listen to what is passing within his own soul? What of the deep solitudes, the distant horizons whose majestic lines seem never to lose their magic power of raising the mind to the level of the great deeds they saw performed? What of the Tiber, with its stern waters, eloquent of the crimes they have engulphed, and the calm of that Roman Campagna through which they roll?

And Rome herself—alone—the triple city, on whose head the centuries have set the proud tiara which her Supreme Pontiff wears—shedding the undying light of Truth, the immortal, over all the earth! What a standpoint! What a noble diapason we have here! What surroundings for the man who knows what meditation means!

Let us have no more flaunting of these equivocal and noisy titles, *naturalism, realism,* and so forth! Art is Nature, yes, *in the first place;* but Nature verified and registered, weighed—*judged,* in a word, before the tribunal of a discernment which analyses, and a reason which rectifies and restores her. Art is a reparation of the failures and forgetfulness of Reality. It is the immortalisation of mortal things by a wise process of elimination, not by a blind and servile worship of their defective and perishable qualities. At all costs and against all comers, then, let us preserve our splendid École de Rome, whose archives bear such names as those of David, Ingres, Flandrin, Regnault, Duret, Hérold, Halévy, Berlioz, Bizet—none of which, as far as I am aware, warrant the scornful pity under which some people would fain wither a dynasty already over a century old.

Let us put forth all our strength to defend the sacred retreat which shelters our growing artist, frees him from premature anxiety concerning his daily bread, and forewarns and forearms him, not against the temptation to mere money-getting only, but against the vulgar triumphs of a paltry and evanescent popularity.

THE ARTIST AND MODERN SOCIETY

THE immense extension of social relations in modern times has had considerable influence on artistic life and work; an influence which, if I mistake not, has done more harm than good.

Formerly, and not so very long ago either, an artist, like a man of learning, was held, and justly so, to be a member of one of the great corporations of intellectual workers. He was looked on as a sort of recluse, whose retreat was sacred from disturbance. Men would have hesitated to tear him from the silence and meditation without which the conception and production of healthy work which will withstand the onslaught of Time—that merciless judge who "never spares aught he did not help to make"—becomes difficult, if not utterly impossible.

Nowadays, the artist is no longer his own master. He belongs to the world at large. He is worse than its target. He is its prey. His own personal and productive life is almost entirely absorbed, swamped, squandered, in so-called social obligations, which gradually stifle him in that network of sham and barren duties which go to make up many an existence devoid of serious object or high motive. In a word, society eats him up.

Now, what is society? It is an aggregation of individuals who are afraid of being bored, and whose sole idea is to get away from their own selves, because of the terror with which the idea of being left in their own sole company inspires them.

Once we begin to tot up the amount of time levied on the artist's working hours by the constantly increasing number of small calls struggling and fighting for his attention all day long, we wonder how, by what extra activity, what effort of concentration, he contrives to perform his chief duty—that of doing honour to the career he has chosen, and to which his best powers and his highest faculties by right belong. It must surely be admitted that in removing the barrier which its scornful indifference, rather than its intelligent discretion, had placed between itself and artists in general, modern society has done them a mischief in no way atoned for by the attractions it offers.

Molière, whose searching glance so deeply fathomed human weaknesses, and who portrayed them with such an unerring hand, addressed the following lines, full of the deepest wisdom and the healthiest philosophy, to the great Colbert:—

> "L'étude et la visite ont leurs talents à part
> Qui se donne à la Cour se dérobé à son art.
> Un esprit partagé rarement s'y consomme
> Et les emplois de feu demandant tout un homme."

Let any one try to realise what can in fairness be expected from the mind of a man incessantly torn hither and thither by evening parties, dinners, perpetual invitations to social gatherings of every sort, a mass of correspondence which leaves him no peace, and the guilty authors of which never dream of saying to themselves, "I am stealing this man's time and thoughts, his very life;" and by all the petty tyrannies, in fine, which go to make up that monster one, called the indiscretion of the public.

And then the visitors, the crowd of idle and curious loungers, who assail your privacy from dawn till dark! Somebody says, "That's all your own fault—you can say you are not at home." Very fine indeed! But how about those letters of introduction, frequently requesting some service on your part which you cannot well refuse? You make up your mind to do your duty, and the visitor is shown in.

"Excuse me; I fear I disturb you!"

"Well, frankly, yes!"

"I beg your pardon; I will not stay now. I'll call another time."

"Oh, pray don't!"

"But—when can I see you without disturbing you?"

"The fact is, I am always busy when I am at home."

"Are you really always so hard at work?"

"Yes, always, unless I am interrupted."

"Oh, I am so sorry to trouble you! But I will only detain you a very few minutes."

"Well, well, sir, that's long enough to kill a man, not to mention an idea! But as you are here, pray proceed."

This is a sample of what occurs daily; and I speak here of artists as a general class. But there is a certain category of artists who have quite special advantages in this line. I can speak out of my own experience, for I refer to musicians. A painter or a sculptor can easily protect his working hours by mercilessly closing his door. He can plead a sitting model, or, if the worst comes to the worst, he can wield the brush or chisel even in the presence of visitors. But the musician? His case is quite different. As his work can be done in daylight, people take his evenings to provide amusement for their guests; and as he can work at night, they come and waste and fritter away his days without the slightest scruple. "And besides," they say, "musical composition is such an easy thing! It is not a matter of labour; it comes of itself, an inspiration!"

My readers cannot have any conception of the innumerable and indiscreet requests to which a musician is daily exposed—the crowds of young pianists, violinists, vocalists, composers, poets (lyric or otherwise), teachers and inventors of various methods, systems and theories, editors of periodicals, pestering you to take their publications; not to mention the requests for autographs, photographs—the albums and the fans, and what not, sent for your signature. It all amounts to a perfect nightmare, and the musician is turned into a sort of national property to which the public has right of access at any and every hour. To be brief, our houses are not in the street any more; the street is in our houses. Our whole life is devoured by idlers, inquisitive folk, loungers who are bored with themselves, and even by *reporters* of all sorts, who force their way into our homes, to inform the public not only as to our private conversation, but as to the colour of our dressing-gowns and the cut of our working-jackets!

Well! That is all wrong, and unhealthy. The precious delicacy, the modesty of feeling, which only lives by quiet contemplation, grows paler and more wilted, day by day, in that unceasing rout, from which the artist brings back nought but a superficial, breathless, feverish activity, tossing convulsively among the ruins of the intellectual balance he has lost for ever.

Farewell to those hours of calm and luminous peace, wherein alone a man can see and hear the workings of his own soul! The noble sanctuary of thought and of emotion, gradually forsaken for the excitements of the outer world, will soon be nothing but a dark and gloomy dungeon, wherein the spirit that knows not how to live in silence must die of weariness.

If the hours thus spent were even not spent in vain! If they were only bestowed on people of some capacity! If they served to cheer none but truly courageous souls!

But think of the waste of time!—the empty conversations. Think of the amount of valueless stuff in that ocean of intercourse, which neither adds nor bestows one tittle of value to the total!

To sum it up, the real plague spot is *the people who are bored,* and who must needs kill other men's time, lest their own should kill them by its weight.

To be bored! To bore one's own self. To try every imaginable dodge to get away from oneself! Is there any poverty in all the world so pitiful as this? And what compensation for that which is bestowed on them can be expected from such a class?

There are certain current opinions, the substance of which people seldom trouble themselves to verify, and which form the huge patrimony of the accepted absurdities. One of these is the belief, the self-persuasion, that the sympathy and protection of the social world are indispensable to an artist's success.

Truly, those who accept such an illusion, and cling to it, must have very little experience of the vivifying atmosphere of a profound artistic conviction.

Social support! It is not uncertain merely; it is the most inconstant, changeable thing on God's earth. And further, it is only given, as a rule, to those who no longer need it, just as the courtiers in a certain famous opera overwhelm a young gentleman, who has just become the recipient of royal favour, with their offers of service. But now that material existence takes the first rank in most men's lives, can we wonder that *seeming* is taken for *being,* and *skilful management* for *talent*? Once the hidden God, the God whose kingdom is within us, is gone from us, we must have idols. Therefore it is that we see so many artists troubled about going here and there and everywhere, leaning on that broken reed of popular advertisement, the fragments of which lie scattered on the weary path of many an uninspired mind and commonplace ambition.

One protection alone is worth the artist's pains, and should be sought by him. His work must be the perfectly sincere expression of his inner feeling. His artistic production must be the outcome of his personal life, the faithful enunciation of his thought. Once that is done, conflicting opinions matter but little to him or it. A work of art can only shed the amount of warmth which has brought it into being, and which it never loses. But the artist must have time to kindle his fire and feed it. Hence a famous composer placed the significant inscription on his door:—

"Those who come to see me do me honour. Those who stay away do me a kindness." In other words, "I am never at home to anybody."

Here, again, is another commonplace, equally popular, and in very frequent use:—

"You'll kill yourself! You work too hard! You really must have some rest! Do come and see us! It will do you good! It will distract your thoughts!"

Distract one's thoughts indeed! Why, that's just what I complain of—what people are much too fond of doing! It's all very well to distract one's thoughts at a set time chosen by oneself. But to have one's thoughts distracted for one, at the wrong time, means to thoroughly confuse them and throw them out of gear.

Work a weariness, an actual danger, forsooth! Those who say so can know very little about it Labour is neither cruel nor ungrateful. It restores the strength we give it a hundredfold, and, unlike your financial operations, the revenue is what brings in the capital.

If there is one incessant worker on the face of God's earth (and He alone knows how various is its toil), it is the heart in man's body. On its regular beat depend not only the continuance of our respiration, but the circulation of our blood, which carries and distributes the different elements necessary to the working of each organ of our frame with such unerring discrimination. This splendid organisation works on incessantly, without a moment's pause, even while we sleep.

Supposing the heart were bidden not to work so hard, to take a little rest—to amuse itself, in short? Now work, to the intellectual life, is what the heart is in our physical life. It is the nourishment, the circulation, the respiration of our intelligence. Like every other sort of gymnastic, it wearies those, and those only, who are not accustomed to it. Work has been described as a punishment, a hardship. It is a healthy and blessed state. Look first at a fertile, well-tilled field, and then at a strip of fallow land? Is not the balance of happiness and charm on the side of cultivation and abundant growth?

It is not labour that kills. It is sterility. To be fruitful is to be young and full of life.

Yet I would not be thought so crotchety, so surly, such a hater of my kind, as to look on an artist as a sort of solitary. It is undoubtedly true, and I willingly acknowledge it, that modern society, in enlarging its borders, has multiplied the artist's opportunities of sharing in various social phases, and meeting many charming and some very useful people.

But what, again, is all that worth, if it costs us those hours of delicious calm—I had almost said of divine hope—when we await (with a longing less frequently disappointed than some would think) the advent of a real emotion, or of some deeply touching truth?

What is all the glare of outside show beside the inner light, serene and glowing, of the beloved Ideal each artist follows without ever wholly reaching it, but which yet draws us on until we feel it loves us more even than we love it?

What then must be the suffering inflicted on the unhappy being torn from a sacred temple and forced into a palace, even were it a thousand times more dazzling than any in the Arabian Nights?

Every one will remember that famous line from one of our greatest poets:

> "Mon verre n'est pas grand, mais je bois dans mon verre."

There is no necessity that every man's cup should be of the same size. The great point is, that each should be always full to the brim. A dwarf, clothed from head to foot in golden raiment, would be just as happy as a giant in similar case, once granting supreme happiness consists in being so attired. This is the ingenious comparison by which St. François de Sales explains how the elect are equal in happiness, even when they are unequal in glory. So apt is it and so subtle, that it may well be applied to every degree in life and every form of perfection.

It is not given to every man to be one of those majestic streams whose waters carry fertility wherever they pass. But the humblest brooklet, if it be pure and limpid, mirrors the sky as faithfully as the mightiest river, or the depths of the ocean itself.

"I will bring her into the wilderness, and speak comfortably unto her," says a Hebrew prophet; and the saintly author of the "Imitation" assures us that "Thy chamber, if thou continuest therein, groweth sweet."

"Well, well!" says somebody else, as though by way of compliment, "it can't be helped. You must pay for being famous!" It is high time the folly of such remarks as this should be exposed. It is a very doubtful advantage, in all conscience, for a man to find himself preyed upon because he is no longer obscure. It cannot be pointed out too often that the artist's *work*, not his *person*, is public property. And there can be no powerful, durable, homogeneous production if his work is to be incessantly mangled and cut up by interruptions. So let society lay to heart the parting counsel given by Molière to the great Minister I have already mentioned:—

> "Souffre que, dans leur art, s'avançant chaque jour,
> Par leurs ouvrages seuls ils te fassent la cour!"

The artist who gives himself up too much to social intercourse runs yet another risk, concerning which it may not be amiss to say a word or two.

By dint of living in the buzz of so many varied opinions, and admirations, and criticisms, and infatuations for some one or other of the fashionable art productions of the moment, he gradually comes to lose confidence in himself, in his own artistic nature, in those dictates of his personal feeling which at one time led him onward, and he ends by finding himself in a hopeless maze. The inner voice which should guide him is lost in the noise of the tempest, and he looks, and looks in vain, to the caprices of a favour that varies with the fashions for a support it is incapable of affording him. Some people say that when you hear a bell strike, you hear only one sound. That depends entirely on the metal and the founding of the bell. If those be perfect, the sound produced is a delightful series of harmonic vibrations.

But what could be more hideous than to hear all the bells in the town strike at once? When, on a thundery day, which makes us feel our breath oppressed and painful, we say "the air is heavy," we use an inappropriate word. The air really is too light. What we call weight is nothing but rarefaction; there is less air than we require to enable us to breathe freely. The same thing applies to the intellectual atmosphere. The man of learning, the artist, the poet, and many beside, each has his own special atmosphere, and must therefore breathe or choke under his own special conditions. Let us not snatch any one of them from his own life-giving element, nor stifle him under what Joseph de Maistre has so well called "the horrible weight of Nothingness."

I know, and I freely confess it, your artist is a being apart, strange, abnormal, whimsical, freakish—an oddity, in fact. Well, grant it all. If his peculiarities cause discomfort, he suffers by them too, and much more, very often, than people think. But, after all, his shortcomings may be forgiven for the sake of what he is, and it may be that his value is owing in part to what he lacks. He must be taken as he is, or left alone. There is no other way to enable him to become all he has it in him to be.

CH. GOUNOD.

THE END.

Lector House believes that a society develops through a two-fold approach of continuous learning and adaptation, which is derived from the study of classic literary works spread across the historic timeline of literature records. Therefore, we aim at reviving, repairing and redeveloping all those inaccessible or damaged but historically as well as culturally important literature across subjects so that the future generations may have an opportunity to study and learn from past works to embark upon a journey of creating a better future.

This book is a result of an effort made by Lector House towards making a contribution to the preservation and repair of original ancient works which might hold historical significance to the approach of continuous learning across subjects.

HAPPY READING & LEARNING!

LECTOR HOUSE

LECTOR HOUSE LLP

E-MAIL: info@lectorhouse.com

9 789356 146914

9 789356 146914

Printed by Libri Plureos GmbH in Hamburg,
Germany